IRELAND'S FINEST
GOLF COURSES

IRELAND'S FINEST
GOLF COURSES

JOHN REDMOND

Gill & Macmillan

CONTENTS

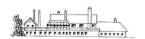

INTRODUCTION

Within the past decade Ireland has become one of the world's premier golfing locations. Its reputation has grown with the development of several outstanding courses that are widely acknowledged to be among the best internationally.

And it is testimony to the quality of this development that Ireland was chosen as host country for the Ryder Cup in 2006.

But for more than a century Ireland could also claim some of the best links courses in the world. It is this combination of the old and the new that has been such an exciting feature of golf in Ireland and that has earned it such widespread recognition.

In this book I have attempted to reveal the modern face of golf in Ireland. Choosing thirty courses to show the superb variety of golfing experience available was not an easy task. So much that is truly excellent had to be omitted (and may well cause some arguments!) But I trust that few readers will disagree that all the courses featured here are worthy of inclusion.

Side by side with the great classics like Portmarnock, Ballybunion, Royal County Down and Lahinch, we have outstanding newcomers like Mount Juliet, Druids Glen, Doonbeg, Old Head, The K Club and many more. Taken all together, I believe that the choice is a fitting tribute to, and celebration of, all that is best in Irish golf.

JOHN REDMOND

ADARE MANOR

HOTEL AND GOLF RESORT

Adare, County Limerick

A new era of luxury styled golf dawned in Ireland when Jack Nicklaus designed Mount Juliet and Arnold Palmer created The K Club. The latest addition is Adare Manor, the brainchild of Robert Trent Jones.

What Jones – the man who had a greater impact than most on golf course architecture since World War Two – has achieved is simply awesome, helped of course by the majestic splendour of the historical 18th century mansion.

A measure of its status is that the handsome Adare Manor Hotel and Golf Resort is rated, outside the USA, as the fourth best resort in the world. The achievement is a fitting salute to the resolute Kane family and how they have created a facility that does so much to boost tourist numbers into the delightful, picture postcard village of Adare, after which the complex is named.

While the sense of luxury knows no bounds at the Manor, the standard of the golf course is similarly

YARDS
7, 135

PAR
72

LOCATION
11 miles/17 km south west
of Limerick to village of Adare.

TYPE
Parkland

EMAIL
reservations@adaremanor.com

WEB
www.adaremanor.com

Thatched cottage in Adare vilage

◀◀ **Stately backdrop**
The historical setting for golf at Adare Manor is amply portrayed by the imposing stately backdrop presented by the Earl of Dunraven's ancestral home, now converted into an award-winning luxury hotel resort.

opulent. Jones demonstrated all his renowned traits in getting the very best from the estate, not least with his canny use of the meandering River Maigue.

Stretching to 7,135 yards off the championship tees (though there is the option of four tees at each hole), Adare has a majestic layout, bearing all the hallmarks of the great designer.

A 14-acre lake dominates the opening nine holes, while the back nine is routed via the relaxing ambience of woodland and river. All the while, however, you will encounter evidence of the Trent Jones trademarks of clover-leaf shaped bunkers, rock-walled babbling streams and those subtle and undulating fairways and greens.

While the 18th hole is acclaimed as Adare's signature, you will thrill to the loop around water from the 4th to the 8th. The back nine also threatens a watery grave, courtesy of the river. This is especially evident at the par three, 11th, along which you get the sensation of apprehension as you edge close to the celebrated finishing hole.

The 18th ▶▶
If ever a hole had the 'wow' factor, this is it, described as 'one of the finest finishing par fives in golf.'
The majestic River Maigue runs ominously the length of the left hand side. To hug that line offers the best opportunity to go for broke and get on the green in two.
The more conservative – and recommended – gambit is to lay up short of the right hand bunkers and then take your rather improved chances of crossing the river to the green. Best to have a spare ball ready!
548 yards
Par 5

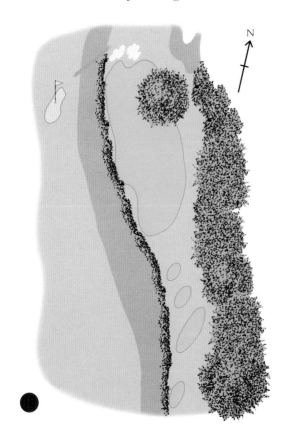

▲ **Water's edge**
The majestic River Maigue meanders
its way amidst the tranquillity but
presents a constant threat alongside
some fairways and greens through
the back nine holes.

◀ The 16th

To achieve a par at the 167 yards, 16th is a proud boast and treasured memory to take away from Adare Manor. A watery grave awaits anything tentatively hit, while to carry the green is to run the risk of finding a difficult resting place in any one of three bunkers.

▼ Finest parkland

The stunning ambience of Adare Manor in the splendidly wooded countryside of County Limerick, shows how architect Robert Trent Jones wove his magic to create one of Ireland's finest parkland courses.

Adare Manor

The history of the magnificent Adare Manor traces its lineage to the mid 1800s when Lady Caroline Wyndham, wife of the second Earl of Dunraven, hatched a fascinating plot. The good Lord Dunraven, crippled with gout, was unable to participate in the familiar activities of a landed gentleman of leisure.

So, Lady Caroline devised the notion of building a new Manor house to occupy her husband with a sense of his own importance. It was a fine idea, as the building of the new house provided labour for the surrounding villagers during the terrible potato famine that devasted Ireland during the mid-19th century.

It is said that the structure is a series of visual allusions to famous Irish and English homes that the Dunravens admired. It is replete with curious eccentricities, such as 52 chimneys to commemorate each week of the year and 365 leaded glass windows to replicate each day of the year!

BALLYBUNION
GOLF CLUB

Sandhills Road, Ballybunion, County Kerry

There can be no more apt or more descriptive introduction to the links at Ballybunion than that of Tom Watson, its greatest admirer and Millennium Year club captain: 'After playing Ballybunion for the first time,' he said, 'a man would think that the game of golf originated here. It is a true seaside links, virtually treeless and a course of sharp contours throughout. There appears to be no man made influence. It looks like a course laid out as it was back in the tenth century. Playing Ballybunion is similar in many respects to playing Cypress Point in America – and I like that style of golf.'

It is uncertain as to who precisely laid out the Old Course, circa 1892. A strong case has been made on behalf of a touring pro named James McKenna. Even Old Tom Morris of St Andrews is mentioned, as is James Braid. History does record that Lionel Hewson and Tom Simpson, did have a major hand in its later development and more recently Tom Watson

OLD COURSE

YARDS
6,598

PAR
71

CASHEN COURSE

YARDS
6,306

PAR
72

LOCATION
1 mile/1.5km south of Ballybunion village

TYPE
Links

EMAIL
bbgolfc@iol.ie

WEBSITE
www.ballybuniongolfclub.ie

himself was invited to make recommendations as to its modernisation.

Ballybunion's reputation was further enhanced by the introduction of a second course, The Cashen. It was designed by the late Robert Trent Jones, the prolific doyen of modern day golf architecture. 'The location is the most natural golf terrain I ever encountered,' he said. This second course ensures that Ballybunion stands apart in terms of a 36-hole links venue of unmatched character and beauty.

The wind blowing in from off the adjacent Atlantic is an almost permanent feature, so you can readily appreciate the sentiments of Watson when he concludes:

'Ballybunion offers some of the finest and most demanding shots on any course I have every played in the world. Combine this with the winds that are prevalent here and you have a magnificent challenge – and that is the character of the place.'

No other comment is required!

◄◄ Unmatched
A broad sweep of the landscape commanded by Ballybunion's Old and New courses, which combine in 36 holes arguably the finest links land holes you will encounter in any one place.

◄ The 16th
The breathtaking view across the par three, 16th green on the New, or Cashen, course, designed by Robert Trent Jones on a piece of land he described as 'the most natural golf course terrain I have ever encountered.'

▲ The 11th
All set for the challenge of the approach to the green on Ballybunion's much chronicled and widely acclaimed feature par four, 11th hole.

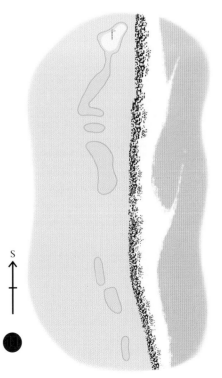

S

◄ The 11th - Old Course
Ballybunion's most photographed hole encapsulates the nature of the links and its picturesque location.
The hole runs alongside the seaside cliff top that is required to be constantly fortified against the threat of coastal erosion caused by the unrelenting Atlantic tides. From a high point tee, the fairway tumbles downwards through the dunes like a staircase and finally to a green at sea level. The 11th is one of three holes at Ballybunion with no bunkers (the other are the 6th and 9th). Don't be complacent and bear in mind it is vital to get a decent drive away.
451 yards
Par 4

Golfing President

The life-size bronze statue of former US President, Bill Clinton, which stands on the entrance to Ballybunion's main street and which was erected on 5 September 1998 to mark the occasion when he played the course.

The 15th ▶
The view from the 15th green which shows Ballybunion's unique setting by the sandy Long Beach. Local legend is that through the haze of the shimmering Atlantic, golfers can behold the vision of Killsaheen, a rare phenomenon consisting of an arch or bridge and the outline of an old woman sitting at a stall selling her wares!

BALLYLIFFIN
GOLF CLUB

Ballyliffin, County Donegal

It is a measure of Ballyliffin golf links that when six times Majors champion Nick Faldo first paid a visit, he was so enchanted that he made an offer to purchase the place!

The discerning members graciously declined. They rightly concurred that you simply could not put a price on – or indeed surrender – what Mother Nature had bestowed on this beautiful corner of Donegal.

If the disappointed Faldo needed compensation (other than being subsequently invited to carry out upgrading to tees, bunkers and greens), then he received it in the interest he unwittingly stirred far beyond Ireland in the Inishowen Peninsula as a location for golf.

Ballyliffin, Buncrana, Portsalon, Rosapenna, Dunfanaghy, North West, Bundoran, Nairn and Portnoo – County Donegal can rival any other region of Ireland as regards golfing riches.

While Faldo was smitten by the Old Links which he described as 'the most natural golf course I have ever seen', what of the subsequent creation

Ballyliffin

OLD LINKS

YARDS
6,615

PAR
71

GLASHEDY LINKS

YARDS
7,217

PAR
72

LOCATION
6 miles/9.5 km from Carndonagh on R238 to Ballyliffin

EMAIL
inf@ballyliffingolfclub.com

WEB
www.ballyliffingolfclub.com

of the accompanying Glashedy course? It is named after the dome-shaped Glashedy Rock that protrudes from the nearby Atlantic on a line from the 12th fairway, and as co-designer Pat Ruddy (in association with the late Tom Craddock), says: it 'graphically represents the enduring spirit of Ballyliffin'.

Given that Ruddy built a masterpiece for himself at The European Club, his legacy to Irish golf architecture is strengthened by Glashedy. It takes account of all the character and charm synonymous with the virtues of links golf, challenging as it does the full repertoire of high and low trajectory shots amid the wonderfully natural dune land.

Glashedy is engaging throughout, marked by a succession of strong par fours to start with, followed by the delight and positioning of its three par threes (not least the quite stunning 5th hole) and the awesome challenge of its three par fives, by consensus, of which the feature hole would be the powerful 15th.

◄◄ **The 13th**

The 13th green on the Glashedy links on a perfect summer's day. The course is an enduring monument to the inspired co-designers Pat Ruddy and the late Tom Craddock.

▼ **Natural golf**

What Mother Nature bestowed and what six times Majors champion Nick Faldo described as 'the most natural golf course I have ever seen.' Faldo was so captivated by what he encountered that he made the members an offer to purchase the course. They declined!

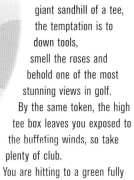

◄ Treasure trove

The classic landscape
at Ballyliffin where
the Old Links and
the newer Glashedy
courses combine in
an exceptional golfing
treasure trove.

◄ ▲ The 7th - Glashedy

Standing on top of a
giant sandhill of a tee,
the temptation is to
down tools,
smell the roses and
behold one of the most
stunning views in golf.
By the same token, the high
tee box leaves you exposed to
the buffeting winds, so take
plenty of club.
You are hitting to a green fully
100 feet below your feet and
where there is no margin for
error, as the green is protected
by a lake on the front right side
and by a pair of devilish pot
bunkers to the left.

183 yards

Par 3

W

21

CARTON HOUSE
GOLF CLUB

Carton, Maynooth, County Kildare

If the hallowed halls of stately Carton House could express their sentiments, you would imagine they would echo approval of how its legend has evolved.

The Carton story has been developing for centuries. And somehow it seems entirely fitting that in this latest chapter, the estate of the ancestral seat of the Earls of Kildare and Dukes of Leinster, should be granted to two latter day giants of golf, for the making of two of Ireland's finest golf courses.

By the hand of leading European player, Colin Montgomerie, 'The Montgomerie' and 'The O'Meara', in salute of top American exponent Mark O'Meara, are woven into the historic landscape, though of conflicting temperament – The Aristocrat and The Temptress, as it were.

The Montgomerie, 7,301 yards, Par 72 is unashamedly the more forbidding. Its renown also centres on a 'links' like feel, as on its more barren, though nonetheless parkland terrain, its fescue

CARTON HOUSE
GOLF CLUB

THE MONTGOMERIE

YARDS
7,301

PAR
72

TYPE
Parkland

THE O'MEARA

YARDS
7,006

PAR
72

LOCATION
14 miles/22km west
of Dublin to Maynooth

TYPE
Parkland

EMAIL
golf@carton.ie

WEB
www.carton.ie

grasses, severe, deep bunkering and firm, fast greens, do at times contrive to simulate the power, pace and appearance of the more traditional seaside courses.

The 3rd and 5th set the stern tone. The 11th, with an equal number of bunkers, maintains it and you will be grateful, too, if you can also cope with the test presented by the dog-legged 16th.

In contrast to Montgomerie's quite uncompromising and severe outline, Mark O'Meara's more permissive design is an expression of how best to sculpt a traditional parkland course amid the rivers, lakes and abundance of ancient oak, beech, cedar and sycamore.

Just tipping the 7,000 yards mark (Par 72), The O'Meara is, in keeping with the personality of the engaging American, a more genteel offering, though of exacting proportions.

The mix is perhaps captured uniquely in Carton's very own 'Amen Corner'. It, too, is a scintillating collection, whereby if you match the par of three-five-three, through the 14th to 16th, you surely will have survived without getting your ball wet!

◄◄ **Serenity**
The serene and distinctive
setting for the Montgomerie
course at Carton – a host venue
for the Irish Open championship.

Carton House ▶
The great halls of stately Carton House,
once the ancestral home of the Earls of
Kildare and Dukes of Leinster, will provide
luxury hotel facilities to complement
appropriately the two fine new golf courses.

◀ **The 15th**
A view on the O'Meara course from the back of the 15th green across to the Shell House which shows the beauty of the mature County Kildare countryside.

▼ **The 15th (The O'Meara)**
Centrepiece of Carton's 'Amen Corner' with an Augusta-like flavour is the fabulous 15th.
A long, sweeping par five highlights the essence of the course, enveloped as it is amid an overhanging tree-lined fairway and bordered from tee to green by the weaving River Rye.
Even allowing for a well-placed drive to avoid bunkers, left and right, the dilemma is which strategy to adopt thereafter: a bold crack at the green over the expanse of the river, or the more cautions three-shot, lay-up strategy?
That is the nature of the beast!
557 yards
Par 5

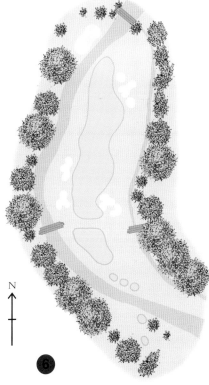

◀ **The 18th**
The boathouse provides an additional feature on the 18th hole of the Montgomerie course and is a stark reminder that any balls hit too far right of the fairway can end up in the Rye Water lake.

N

CONNEMARA
GOLF CLUB

Ballyconeely, Clifden, County Galway

It is a proud boast of the Connemara championship links that the par of 72 is seldom matched and rarely beaten.

On the one hand, the distracting beauty of the location might be a contributing factor. More probable would be the interminable wind from the Atlantic and its effect on Ireland's most westerly championship links.

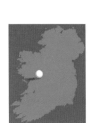

Close to where the intrepid aviators Allcock and Brown found safe landing after their pioneering trans-Atlantic flight in June 1919, the Connemara course is remote. It is nestled between the scenic splendour of the Twelve Bens mountain range and the rugged Atlantic Ocean. It is an enduring monument to its designer Eddie Hackett.

The unveiling in the year 2000 of an additional nine holes hugging the sea shore, adds a further dimension to a much sought after venue for the many visitors who wisely put the bustling resort town of Clifden on their holiday itinerary.

YARDS
7,055

PAR
72

TYPE
Links

LOCATION
8 miles/12.8 km
west of Clifden

E-MAIL
links@iol.ie

WEB
www.connemaragolflinks.com

Roundstone Harbour

Eddie Hackett graciously acknowledged that the rugged landscape of Connemara contributed greatly to the success of the design. His deft ability to enhance what nature presented him results in a dramatic championship course, ready-made to tempt those who savour beauty – and a beast!

'If there was a course like this on the west coast of England, it would surely host the British Open championship,' said Peter Alliss when he first played Connemara.

◄◄ Rugged terrain
The rugged, rocky terrain at Ballyconeely from which was crafted Ireland's most westerly championship links.

Inspired locations ►
While Connemara is built mainly on flat ground, some higher land allowed architect Eddie Hackett to vary the lay out with inspired locations for some greens.

▼ The 13th
Connemara's most talked of hole is the par three, 13th on the championship course. It has many virtues, not least its beautiful setting, as the links builds to its notoriously demanding crescendo. Perhaps it's more prudent to opt to play off a more forward tee, as this awesome 'one-shotter' is essentially a do-or-die challenge across the vast uncharted chasm from tee to green.
215 yards
Par 3

N

▲ Imposing backdrop
The Twelve Bens stand as an imposing and picturesque mountainous backdrop to the scenic Connemara links.

The 18th ►
Connemara's 18th hole, at the mercy of winds invariably whipping in from the adjacent Atlantic, provides an exhilarating climax.

COUNTY LOUTH
GOLF CLUB

Baltray, County Louth

The ultimate recognition of County Louth golf club was its nomination as the venue for the Irish Open championship. But quite why it took until 2004 to be conferred with such an honour is a mystery.

Perhaps part of its mystique was that Baltray, the name of the local village by which the course is better known, jealously protected its privacy, happily ensconced in its own treasured isolation.

Amid some classic dunescape and by the River Boyne winding its way to the Irish Sea, the County Louth Club has an enduring sense of history. Much of this is associated with families bearing such proud golfing names as Reddan, Garvey, McGurk, Smyth and Gannon.

Especially notable has been the impact made by two lady golfers, Clarrie Reddan and Philomena Garvey. And don't forget the Ryder Cup star, Des Smyth.

YARDS
6,936

PAR
72

LOCATION
5 miles/8km east
of Drogheda

TYPE
Links

E-MAIL
baltray@indigo.ie

WEB
www.countylouthgolfclub.com

Melifont Abbey

And to think it all started by chance in 1892 when G.H. Pentland and John Gilroy laid out a few holes in the dunes (much to the displeasure of the local inhabitants!). Their work was completed by a Scottish professional with the curious name of Snowball. Thirty years later Tom Simpson (who had been involved in the development of Ballybunion) updated the original design and gave us the magnificent course that we know today.

It speaks highly of Simpson's enduring design that when Baltray was modernised in 1983 they only had to tinker with the original. Several new tees were added to introduce some additional venom and the course was extended to 6,936 yards.

Two par fives in the opening three holes sets a tone, while an acclaimed chain of par fours between the 12th and 14th is at the heart of the wonderful challenge laid down by this truly classic course.

◄◄ Golfing gem
County Louth, or Baltray as it is also fondly known, is a golfing gem set amid isolated and classic dune land and by the River Boyne.

▲ The 14th
The exciting challenge of the second nine holes at County Louth is encapsulated in the holes close to the sea, which combine accurate driving, second shots between narrow gaps in the dunes and the intriguing challenge of the short par four, 14th, just one of Baltray's many fine features.

Championship status ►
County Louth's delights are many and endless. Some revisions made in the 1930s by Tom Simpson brought the course to championship status.

▼ **Bestowed by Nature**
A graphic example of County Louth's natural setting amid towering sand dunes and some murderous rough.

▼▼ **The 13th**
The 13th par four of 421 yards is known as 'Manx Men's Gap' in honour of the crew of a ship from the Isle of Man which ran aground beside the fairway during a storm in the last century. This quality hole is a highlight of the back nine.

14th hole ▶
An intriguing four which highlights some of the excitement of the back nine. The drive is from a high tee offering superb views of a magnificent expanse of golden beach with the Mourne Mountains in the background. The instinct is to go for a booming drive so as to minimise the club for the second shot that demands delicate precision, as the relatively small, plateau green slopes pronouncedly on three sides.

332 yards
Par 4

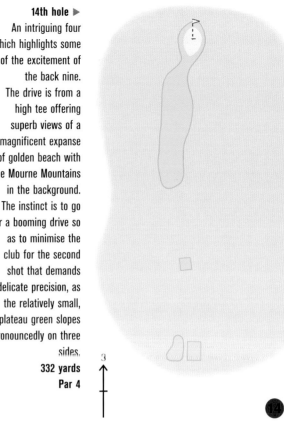

33

COUNTY SLIGO
GOLF CLUB

Rosses Point, County Sligo

The links at County Sligo golf club at Rosses Point are a splendid example of how superlatively a course can be conceived when the surrounding landscape is included as part of the overall design concept.

This is hardly surprising when the eye-catching design was that of Harold Colt, in the early 1920s. Immortalised as the first outstanding golf architect who had not previously been a professional golfer, Colt took full advantage from the landscape with which he was presented in one of the most scenically beautiful areas of Ireland.

We have marvelled at his work ever since, taking account of its setting beneath the immense Ben Bulben headland on the one side and by the panorama over Dead Man's Point westward to the Atlantic Ocean.

The local inhabitants of Rosses Point village (after which name the club is more popularly known) are enormously proud of the magnificent course on their doorstep. Since 1923, they have played host to the players of the West of Ireland championship.

YARDS
6,647

PAR
71

LOCATION
5 miles/8 km north
of Sligo town
to Rosses Point village.

TYPE
Links

EMAIL
jim@countysligogolfclub.ie

WEB
www.countysligogolfclub.com

Ben Bulben

Leading golfer and commentator Peter Alliss has written that 'people will come away marvelling at its beauty'. For Tom Watson: 'Rosses Point is amongst my favourite links'. Bernhard Langer is another admirer who came to play one round and stayed for a fortnight.

Standing on the high rise green at the 2nd hole reveals the infinite beauty of the place. Thereafter, as you wend your way around its rolling fairways and cliff top plateaux – looking out for meandering streams – you will be engrossed by what you see.

County Sligo's scenic best is far out towards Ben Bulben in the distinguishing loop between the 9th and 13th holes.

Enjoy the peace if you can, because once you turn hard left for home along the sea shore, you are required to run the gauntlet of whatever weather is rushing in from the Atlantic.

Your mood can change dramatically as you grapple with the rousing climax of the final four holes. Any par is to be treasured.

◄◄ **Immortalised by Yeats**
The breathtaking setting at Rosses Point beneath the immense backdrop of 'bare Ben Bulben's head', as Yeats called the mountain, and alongside Dead Man's Point westward to the Atlantic Ocean.

▼ **The 2nd**
The infinite beauty of golf at Rosses Point is superbly illustrated by the scenic views from the high rise green of the 2nd hole.

▲ **Yeats Country**

'The Land of Heart's Desire'
was how the poet W.B.Yeats
described County Sligo, as seen
here across the Rosses Point
links reaching out to 'Bare Ben
Bulben's Head' and the area of
Drumcliffe Church, where the
great poet lies buried.

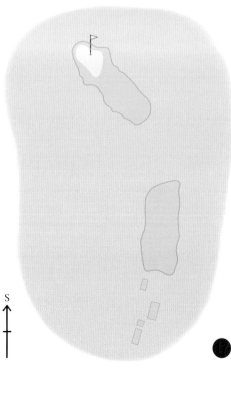

S

◄ **The 17th - The Gallery**

Aptly named 'The Gallery' as the green nestles
beneath the craggy face of a hillock which is
frequently used as a viewing platform.
A brilliant design concept covers 414 rising yards.
The drive calls for controlled accuracy.
You must be short of some rough terrain so as to
have the reasonable chance of a second shot off
level ground aimed high and long to the raised and
tilting green. Not easy!

Par 4

414 yards

DOONBEG
GOLF CLUB

Doonbeg, County Clare

There was rich reward in re-tracing the footsteps of history. It led to the creation of Doonbeg Golf Club.

The story dates back to 1892 when officers of the Scottish Black Watch Regiment realised they had discovered an ideal location for links golf. However, they chose to play at nearby Lahinch, because of its accessibility to the old West Clare railway line.

A century later, just as you imagined that there could be no more links sites available in Ireland, the pages of history reveal something long forgotten. Doonbeg is now of such astounding quality that it has already been compared with the best. It is a tribute to Greg Norman, its inspirational designer.

Doonbeg is set on 1.5 miles of beach and dune. Views of the Atlantic can be enjoyed from sixteen of the eighteen holes. Some of the dunes soar to 100 feet. And designer Norman says that fourteen of Doonbeg's greens and twelve of its fairways presented themselves so naturally that he was able to readily indulge his 'least disturbance' design philosophy.

DOONBEG GOLF CLUB

YARDS
6,870

PAR
72

LOCATION
40 miles/64kms from
Shannon International
Airport on N 67 to
village of Doonbeg

TYPE
Links

EMAIL
dooonbeggolfclub@eircom.net

WEB
www. Doonbeggolfclub.com

Cliffs of Moher

Such was the compatibility of the terrain that enthusiasts of the game wonder if, in fact, the land discovered does not endure as 'the last great piece of links land on the West coast of Ireland?'

Nature spontaneously throws up countless fine holes, and while there may be balmy, sun-drenched days, in these exposed parts the temperamental weather clerk will also dispense his displeasures.

One stark illustration would be the seemingly 'giveaway' 14th hole. It measures a mere 111 yards. Yet it can play anything from a sand wedge to a five-iron.

In point of fact, there is the feeling that Doonbeg might be that bit too severe, although in mere length it comes in well under the 7,000 yards benchmark. Norman makes no apologies.

It's well worth the journey west to find out why, and bring a camera to record the visit. You will certainly want to go away with keepsakes of the 1st, 9th, 14th, 15th and 18th for a start.

◀◀ **The 6th**

The stunning par four, 6th hole, which runs alongside the Atlantic on an undulating, deep-bunkered fairway, flanked by plentiful marram grasses.

▲ **The 4th**

Sunset helps to show the wonderfully natural links character of the 4th hole which features many deep-faced pot bunkers that are so synonymous with the links.

The 7th ▶

The 7th is nestled in an amphitheatre of smaller dunes framing the hole as seen from the back tee from which, on a clear day, you can see the Cliffs of Moher.

▲▶ The 8th

The most difficult hole on the course, a three shot par five if ever there was one. It captures the very essence of the location, your third shot being into the prevailing winds and into the backdrop of the Atlantic. It takes three great shots to reach the huge expanse of green which throws up tough, challenging undulations. A par is to be treasured.

582 yards
Par 5

N

Enjoy!

'The ultimate links golf experience' is how they market Doonbeg. You will surely concur.

Part of the appeal has been built in the experience and camaraderie, as much as how you play. 'Leave your pencil in your bag and enjoy the moment', is the Invitation.

In addition to the adventure of playing the unique links, the off-course extras truly set the place apart, as locker room, clubhouse and a 19th hole Pub are augmented by a luxury village-styled setting of suite and cottage accommodation.

▼ The 13th
The par five 13th hole, which is an understandable favourite with golfers and photographers alike.

The 10th ▶
The wonderful 10th hole, where creative architect Greg Norman, offers a tempting choice of risk and reward to a sunken green nestling in a dune hollow.

DROMOLAND CASTLE
HOTEL AND COUNTRY ESTATE

Newmarket on Fergus, County Clare

Dromoland Castle is renowned the world over as one of Ireland's finest Castle hotels. Now it has a golf course equally fit for a king – and his queen.

Watched over by the baronial splendour of the 16th century five-star hotel, this is a representation of ancient history meeting the 21st century. The new golf course is one of Ireland's finest in a parkland setting.

Such a seamlessly complementary fusion is courtesy of the renowned US architect Ron Kirby, in association with the late and great Irish amateur Joe Carr. It is immediately evident that Dromoland can take its place alongside such other legendary south western courses as Lahinch, Ballybunion, Tralee and Waterville.

The eighteen enchanting holes are carved from a delightful sweep of woodland, open pasture, lakes and streams. Its ambience is further enriched by plentiful flora and fauna. Deer, pheasant and other wildlife abound within the estate.

Completed in 2003, measuring 6,845 yards

DROMOLAND CASTLE

YARDS
6,845

PAR
72

LOCATION
1 mile/1.6 km north of
Newmarket on Fergus,
On N18

TYPE
Parkland

EMAIL
golf@dromoland.ie

WEB
www.dromoland.ie

O'Brien's Tower, Cliffs of Moher

and in keeping with the luxury standards of the internationally renowned hotel, the course is built to the highest benchmark specifications of the United States Golf Association. Firm, fast putting surfaces are the norm.

Played largely against the crenellated magnificence of the imposing castle, the challenge is both easy on the eye and testing in the playing. Examples are plentiful on the beguiling journey. Water is potentially in play at half the holes whether it is the meandering River Rine or the formidable Lough Dromoland.

Classic examples are the par three 7th, hitting straight on a line to the castle, overlooking the lake; the 11th, a double dog-leg beginning with a tee shot requiring a carry of fully 200 yards over marshland; the exquisite short 17th across the pond and then around to the tee for the formidable par five, 18th tee. It is set back amid the reeds and asks for another big carry across the corner of the lake.

Plenty of risk. Lots of reward. Dromoland is indeed a world apart.

◄◄ The 7th

The 7th at Dromoland is a charming par three of great visual beauty and shows how a castle dating from the sixteenth century (and now a five star hotel) can blend with the best of 21st century course design.

◄ Woodland marsh and lake

A fine evening moves towards dusk on one of Ireland's most acclaimed new parkland courses.

◄▲ The 18th

The sense of foreboding on the tee is confirmed by the challenge of a 200 yards plus carry to beat the marshland and reach the apron of the fairway. It's another big hit towards the castle to get sight of the green, rather concealed by the large and rare Monterey cypress as if on protective sentry duty.
This is a three-shotter, the final pitch requiring a touch of perfection away from the left hand bunker on a sharply contouring green. A magnificent finish.

572 yards

Par 56

S

18

47

DRUIDS GLEN
GOLF CLUB

Newtownmountkennedy, County Wicklow

Hardly had the paintwork dried on the magnificent landscape that is Druids Glen, than co-designer Pat Ruddy was challenged with the task of matching his original brief to create 'Ireland's best inland course'.

The end product is the emergence of an adjoining little sister, named Druids Heath and the choice of which one is the more comely is left to yourself!

Of what there is no doubt is that the combination of the two courses — adorned by the magnificent Marriott Hotel complex — adds up to what is unquestionably one of Europe's finest golf resorts.

Situated just a forty-minute drive from Dublin city down the scenic east coast, we have the golfer's equivalent of the Garden of Eden. It presents itself as a fitting monument to the new face of Irish golf and also to the architectural genius of designer Ruddy, Ireland's finest of his generation.

It was a measure of the recognition of Druids Glen that within one year of its opening in 1995,

Geann na bRaoice

DRUIDS GLEN

YARDS
7,046

PAR
71

DRUIDS HEATH

YARDS
7,434

PAR
71

LOCATION
N 11 to
Newtownmountkennedy

TYPE
Druids Glen – Parkland
Druids Heath – Heath/Links

E-MAIL
info@druidsglen.ie

WEB
www.druidsglen.ie

it was deemed of sufficient merit to host the Irish Open championship.

Compared to the rich parkland setting of the Glen, the Heath's layout embodies a contrasting heathland/links texture, set as it is amid plentiful gorse, rock quarries, with trademark pot bunkers and, of course, a testing sea breeze.

The traditional links feel is especially evident at two tantalising par threes. Firstly at the uphill 5th where you will long to pull out that all too infrequent Sunday-best and then at the downhill 11th, where, if you can divert your eyes away from the splendour of the distant Sugarloaf mountain, you might concentrate on the immediate task in hand.

By any standard the courses have unfolded as two of Ireland's best, acclaimed by the Ryder Cup duo, Colin Montgomerie and Sergio Garcia, as they were crowned Irish Open champions.

At his first glance, fellow Ryder Cup ace, Eamonn Darcy exclaimed: 'They have created a complete litany of great holes — I think it is superb'.

◄ **The 8th**
The striking par three, 8th hole's colourful backdrop of forests and streams captures beautifully the very essence of Druids Glen, a fabulous golfing sanctuary in County Wicklow, known as the Garden of Ireland.

Landscaping and attention to horticultural detail is at the root of Druids Glen's virtues. The eye-catching tone is especially evident at the par three 8th and 12th holes, both across water. Similarly at the magnificent par four 18th where the green is fronted by not one, not two, but three sparkling lakes, cascading over granite stone walls. Awesome!

The 12th ▶
The mystically named Druids Glen originates from the fact that a Druids Altar – a preserved stone altar of pre-Christian worship – stands on the wooded hillside over looking the 12th green.

▼ Rural splendour
The pastoral scene for the 9th hole embraces the spectacular location commanded by the newer Druids Heath course beneath the outline of the Wicklow Mountain range.

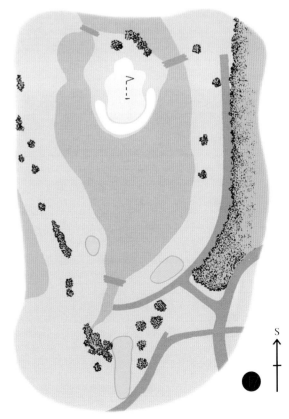

▲ **Soulful**
The exquisite setting for the par four, 6th hole on Druids Heath seems amply to capture the sentiments of course designer Pat Ruddy: 'Dull would he be of soul who would allow a few stray golf shots spoil a day in such a blessed spot!'

The 17th ▶
Take a deep breath; you are negotiating one of the most notorious holes in Irish golf. Length alone indicates the severity of the challenge. It's a white knuckle ride at the most critical point of the course. Your task is somehow to traverse a whopping expanse of lake to an island green. First it's how and then by how many!
Par 3
203 yards

S

51

THE EUROPEAN CLUB

Brittas Bay, County Wicklow

YARDS
7, 368

PAR
72

LOCATION
35 miles / 56 km
South east of Dublin city
to Jack White's Inn

TYPE
Links

EMAIL
info@theeuropeanclub.ie

WEB
www.theeuropeanclub.com

St Kevin's Church, Glenadlough

When you consider that the curriculum vitae of Pat Ruddy is adorned with the designs of so many other highly acclaimed courses, you get an inkling of the architectural merit of what he built for himself at The European Club.

The classic Glashedy links at Ballyliffin, the wonders of the two courses at Druids Glen, the merit of St. Margaret's and update work carried out on County Donegal's famous Murvagh, Portsalon and Rosapenna links, sets Ruddy apart. The European Club may well be the pièce de résistance.

The first major golf links to be developed on Ireland's eastern seaboard in over one hundred years, The European Club has won world-wide acclaim. A showcase of how best a design can be integrated with a landscape of classic dune along the seashore, it includes the four ball of Tiger Woods, Mark O'Meara, David Duvall and Scott McCarron amongst its many eulogisers. Woods, in fact, was so inspired that on his visit in July 2002,

as US Masters and the US Open champion, he prepared for his defence of the British Open by establishing a links record of 67. He was promptly made an honorary member.

Added value at The European Club is that you can play 20 holes! So as to fully utilise all the merits that nature intended, two loops of 10 holes have been built. Innovation is in keeping with the romantic nature of designer-owner Ruddy. Thus you get the bonus of two superb par threes, located between the 7th and 8th holes and again between the 12th and 13th holes.

The scenic stretch from the 7th to the 14th seems to capture the very heart of the links. It comprises six very substantial par fours, all over 400 yards, followed by a bone-crunching par five of 596 yards along the edge of the sea.

Endorsements of The European Club's virtues are many. A consortium of magazines led by Golf (USA) and Golf Monthly (UK) included the club's 7th amongst the World's Greatest 100 Holes and the 13th and 14th amongst the World's 500 Greatest.

◄◄ **The 3rd**
A combination of rugged dunes, deep bunkers, sea views, undulating fairways and greens at the 3rd hole capture the very spirit of The European Club at Brittas Bay.

▲▼ **The 7th**
This hole probably best illustrates Ruddy's design concept.
A river hugs the fairway to the green all the way on the right hand side.
The left hand flank offers no relief. It is 'jungle country' most of the way, with a protruding reed-filled marsh halfway, adding to the terror.
Be respectful. This is Index 1 – and for good reason.
470 yards
Par 4

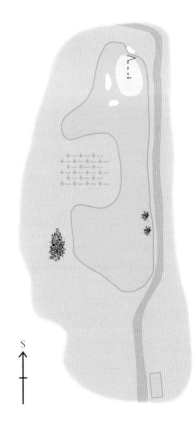

S

◄ **The 8th**
The magnificent par four 8th hole with tumbling fairways amid the dune valleys and flanked by the Irish Sea.

▲ **The 11th**
At 416 yards and heading towards the Irish Sea the 11th hole is strategically set at the very heart of the challenge provided by this links.

Roll of Honour

A unique element of golf at The European Club – and, a measure of the esteem with which the links and its owner-designer Pat Ruddy are held – is the numbers of holes commemorating great champions of the game. Players were invited to nominate the type of golf hole by which they wished to be remembered. The following dedications in whose honour golfers are exhorted to play that hole with the spirit of the champion concerned are: -

Sam Snead - 4th hole *(Par 4)*
Peter Thomson - 5th hole *(Par 4)*
Lee Trevino - 6th hole *(Par 3)*
Arnold Palmer - 7th hole *(Par 4)*
Fred Daly (pictured) - 8th hole *(Par 4)*
Gary Player - 11th hole *(Par 4)*
Billy Casper - 12th hole *(Par 4)*
Tony Jacklin - 13th hole *(Par 5)*
Gene Sarazen - 14th hole *(Par 3)*
Johnny Miller - 16th hole *(Par 4)*
Tom Watson - 17th hole (Par 4)

▲ **The 14th**
The unforgiving par three 14th, a favourite of the legendary Gene Sarazen, to whom this exquisite hole is dedicated.

GALGORM CASTLE

Galgorm Road, Ballymena, County Antrim

As if stoutly making the statement that Northern Ireland has not been found wanting in contributing to Ireland's new golfing image, the grandiose Galgorm Castle has emerged as a shining symbol of all that is the very best in contemporary golf.

Since the early 1990s, the Ulster counties have blossomed with countless new courses. But few have

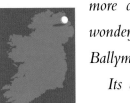

more character and presence than this wonderful creation on the outskirts of Ballymena by the lovely glens of Antrim.

Its charm has its origins in a 400-years-old estate on which stands one of Ireland's historic castles, built in 1618 by the eccentric Sir Faithful Fortescue.

Its present day owner-occupier is Christopher Brooke, the enterprising grandson of one of Northern Ireland's former prime ministers, Lord Brookeborough.

A generous budget has yielded the rich dividend of a top drawer contemporary layout. The

YARDS
6,736

PAR
72

LOCATION
Outskirts of Ballymena,
20 miles/32 km north
of Belfast

TYPE
Parkland

EMAIL
golf@galgormcastle.com

WEB
www.galgormcastle.com

Giant's Causeway, County Antrim

course is constructed to the highest specifications and blends harmoniously into a mature old world atmosphere bounded by the Rivers Maine and Braid. Five lakes also contribute to the picture postcard setting.

There can hardly be a more inspiring location for a game of golf. With the backdrops of the castle and the ancient Irish fort of the MacQuillan clan, the variety of holes is immense. The 3rd, 7th, 14th and 17th are good examples.

Water is everywhere! At the 3rd it's right and left of the tee to start with. At the 7th anything short and right will end up in the water. The 14th is bounded by the river and at the 17th you need to hug a right hand line to stay clear of the stream.

Adding to the attractiveness of a visit to Galgorm Castle is its proximity to such tourist attractions as the Giant's Causeway and the Glens of Antrim, making it an ideal base from which to explore some of the scenic delights of Northern Ireland.

◄ The 15th
The special character
of one of Northern
Ireland's finest new golf
courses has been
created in an historic
estate, close by the
lovely glens of Antrim.

N

▲ **The 4th**
The challenging view from
the 4th tee where water
must be carried before
approaching the green.

◄ **The 15th**
Imperative to take a lefthand
route on a hole where you have
three chances of being in the water!
Be forewarned, the lengthy stretch of
lake on the right can not be seen from
the tee.
For the pitch shot to the green, bear in
mind you are hitting to a raised surface
and there are two mischievous bunkers
to the front right, awaiting the
indecisive.
382 yards
Par 4

▲ **1618 castle**
At the heart of Galgorm's charm one of Ireland's
historically unique castles, built in 1618, stands
like a stern sentinel.

▲ **The 14th**
The green at the par three 14th hole where locals will advise you to 'aim at the Slemish Mountains on the horizon – and be sure to take plenty of club!'

◀ **The 7th**
Another of Galgorm's par three treasures. The tee at the 141 yards, 7th, presents a deceptive challenge where any balls hit short and right of the green could find a watery grave.

THE HERITAGE

Killenard, County Laois

Seve Ballesteros has left an indelible mark on Irish golf. Firstly, by his memorable and colourful performances as three times Irish Open champion; secondly, as the inspiration behind one of the country's finest courses.

What he has created at The Heritage, in association with the Irish-Canadian designer Jeff Howse, is nothing short of astounding. Packaged with an extraordinarily handsome clubhouse, hotel and resort, his achievement is one of the finest all-in golfing facilities in Europe.

In addition to golf, this wonderland also includes the largest indoor bowls stadium in the country. You can purchase a home here and you can even indulge your tastes and wet the whistle at a traditional Irish thatched pub which makes for a unique 19th hole.

The opulent nature of the surroundings is matched by the scale of a course spread generously through a maturing plantation.

YARDS
7,319

PAR
72

LOCATION
40 miles/65km south
of Dublin on M7 to
Killenard village

TYPE
Parkland

EMAIL
info@theheritage.com

WEB
www.theheritage.com

Rock of Dunamase

◄◄ The 18th
A view from behind the 18th green shows vividly how co-designers Seve Ballesteros and Jeff Howse seamlessly integrated one of Ireland's most acclaimed contemporary course designs into the landscape.

The 10th ►
A large bunker complex protects the green at the 10th hole, a left to right dog-leg par five, where you are offered a-risk-or-reward strategy.

▼ The 6th
Bunkers await on both sides of the fairway to penalise errant tee shots.
There is a stream in play 50 yards short of the green for the second shot.
Take note also that the green is well protected, by a lake on the left and by a string of spacious bunkers on the right.
455 yards
Par 4

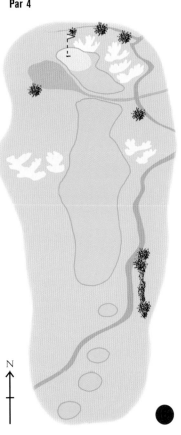

No two holes seem to be similar in design and central to the challenge is that you must plot your course safely around one hundred lavishly-contoured bunkers and ten acres of artificial lakes.

The Heritage will leave you with the fondest of memories and the sweetest of tastes.

◄ **The 19th**
The handsome
clubhouse, hotel and
leisure resort makes for
one of the finest 19th
hole facilities you will
encounter anywhere.

▲ **The 17th**
The demanding par
three 17th at 195 yards
requires an accurate
long iron, or even a wood.
Don't be short!

◄ **The 8th**
The attractively set 8th green is another reminder that sand and water are constantly to hand. The design presents a tempting second shot but think long and hard before you take it.

Improving your skills

Along with lending his name to the design of The Heritage course, Seve Ballesteros also provided the Ballesteros 'natural' golf school. It is only the third in the world, after Spain and Japan, and takes special account of the short game, for which the great Spaniard is renowned.

Central to the school's philosophy is The Swing Room, incorporating digital video technology, a bio mechanics room, an indoor putting green and club custom fitting.

THE ISLAND
GOLF CLUB

Corballis, Donabate, County Dublin

The appointment of The Island golf club as Ireland's on-going regional qualifying course for the British Open Championship, lets the cat out of the bag!

Such an association with one of the four major events of world golf, suggests an exposure and profile never previously experienced – and it's not before time.

For too long, this quaint and endearing old club has been left in the shadows of its more famous links neighbours along the east coast.

Originally reached only by boat across a narrow estuary, the club became more accessible when a road was built. Nonetheless, The Island remained remote and largely unknown and unappreciated, despite its great qualities.

This seemed unjust given its place in history and the merits of the design work carried out by Harold Hilton, early golf's most famous amateur, who also earned a reputation as a course architect. His style and tone have been preserved in the main, with updating and adjustment and the seamless

YARDS
6,823
PAR
71
LOCATION
15 miles/24 km north
of Dublin city, off M1
TYPE
Links
E-MAIL
info@islandgolfclub.com
WEB
www.theislandgolfclub.ie

The old mainland jetty

introduction of some new holes carved out of the dunes. In the words of European PGA tour giant Darren Clarke: 'The Island is a fantastic links, which tests every club in the bag.'

The history and tradition of the links are evidenced in the quaint titles originally attributed to the holes; Broadmeadow (a classic Par 3), the Andes (another great one-shotter), the Prairie (an exemplary links Par 5) and the Cricket Field.

The reasonably subdued front nine plays as a foretaste to what unfurls as a magnificent mix through classic duneland on the loop home. For instance, the only two par fives on the course – the Quarry at No. 10 and the Prairie at No. 15 – dare you to underestimate the length of the challenge. So you will know you have been in a fight!

The Island's place in history goes back to 1890, when, by chance, it was discovered by a group of male friends wanting, as was the growing trend at the time, to learn more about the increasingly popular game called golf.

Having taken a lease of the land, they set about forming a club whose members were confined to their bachelor friends! This single-sex status turned out to be short-lived as it was the ladies, upon their acceptance in 1910, who quickly blazed the trail for The Island by their many successes in various women's championships.

Legend has it that the immortal cricketer W. G. Grace once played on the course. The club's colourful history recalls that Grace and some friends came to the Island to play golf, whereupon the members threw down an additional challenge to play cricket.

It is said that Grace was bowled out first ball and the 11th hole is now named after him.

◀◀ The 13th
'The Island is a fantastic links' attests Ryder Cup ace, Darren Clarke, in salute of a true links where the original design work of the famous Harold Hilton has largely been preserved down through the generations.

From the air ▶
View from the air of the precious junction of land discovered by chance in 1890 and which subsequently evolved as a quaint and endearing golf links of the highest quality.

▲ The 3rd
Possibly the toughest of the par fours. Requires absolute accuracy, especially with second shot, as the approach and two tier green tend to throw ball off to the right. Watch out for the hidden greenside bunker on left.

◄ Hills and plains
The green of The Prairie (the 15th) with the tee of The Andes (the 16th) in the background.

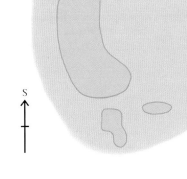

◄ The 13th - Broadmeadow
A classic Par 3 hard by the sea- shore across Broadmeadow Estuary and where your fate is determined by the weather.

It's 211 yards back to 'the mainland' so you will need plenty of ammunition: firstly, in the choice of club – take an extra one – and maybe too in the number of balls you have in your bag! Heed the advice of local Ryder Cup hero, Philip Walton, who says: 'Clear the large grass bunker which guards the green and you may be rewarded with a birdie. The alternative is to play safe down the left side and then chip on'.
Par 3
211 yards

THE K CLUB

Straffan, County Kildare

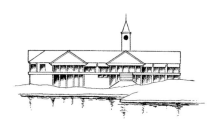

The nomination of The K Club as venue for Ryder Cup 2006 realised a joyful ending to a shared dream of businessman Dr. Michael Smurfit and legendary golfer/designer Arnold Palmer.

When they unveiled this quite stunning and luxurious complex back in the early 1990s, the hosting of the first ever Ryder Cup in Ireland was a declared ambition.

All of Ireland should now reap the benefits, as never previously has a representation of the country's golf brand been subjected to such exposure as that centred on the thirty-sixth Ryder Cup matches.

The Kildare Hotel and County Club, to give it its full and grandiose title, is itself a representation of the new opulent face of Irish golf. It has two courses, the Palmer and the Smurfit.

'We could draw for 100 years and still not come up with as good a vision again' is Arnold Palmer's judgment that is widely endorsed.

PALMER'S COURSE

YARDS
7,212

PAR
72

TYPE
Parkland

SMURFIT COURSE

YARDS
7,277

PAR
72

TYPE
Parkland

LOCATION
20 miles / 32 km south-west of Dublin city on N4/M4 to Straffan village.

EMAIL
golf@thekclub.ie

WEB
www.kclub.ie

It is difficult not to concur, given what Palmer achieved on a beautiful spread of countryside in the heart of County Kildare, just down the road from the famous Curragh racecourse and National Stud.

Because of its association with the Ryder Cup, the Palmer course inevitably commands centre stage. It has long been described as the greatest and toughest inland golf course in Ireland.

Be forewarned that water is one prominent element of its taxing challenge. It can come into play on as many as fourteen holes. Decorative and tactically placed lakes abound and the River Liffey, which meanders for one mile through the property, borders the 7th, 8th, 16th and 17th.

As if not altogether fulfilled by the building of one internationally acclaimed course, the inspired Smurfit and Palmer combination then created a stunning second course named the Smurfit. On adjoining land, it presents another great, though distinctly different, challenge.

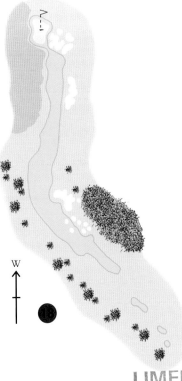

◄◄ Palmer's Delight
Grandly acclaimed as 'the ultimate finishing hole', the 18th on the Ryder Cup, Palmer course is marked by the presence of much water and plentiful sand.

◄ The 16th
Viewed from the back of the green, the infamous 16th is probably the most intimidating hole on the Ryder Cup course. The green can be reached only by traversing a daunting stretch of lake, at a point where swirling winds can play wicked tricks.

▲ The 17th
The pivotal par three, 17th hole alongside the River Liffey carries the double threat of a watery grave on the one side and a sandy burial ground on the other. You'll graciously accept par!

The 18th ►
The crowning glory to Arnold Palmer's spectacular design. Brilliantly conceived as the ultimate finishing hole and made for the Ryder Cup climax beneath the clubhouse verandah. A true gallery favourite. Possible to eagle and birdie, but susceptible to bogey – and more - it dares you throughout. Firstly, it defies you off the drive to take the tight line over the bunker-strewn hill. It then provokes you to go for broke and aim straight at the flag, invariably tucked behind the water's edge of the great expanse of lake that runs in front of and beside the green. Mere mortals should lay up in a three shot tactic designed to combat a high risk card wrecker.

537 yards
Par 5

Commemorative stamp

To commemorate the staging of the 36th Ryder Cup in the K Club in 2006, An Post, the Irish Postal Service, issued four stamps. Three of the stamps feature Irish players who played in teams that won or retained the Ryder Cup. The fourth stamp features a view from the clubhouse overlooking the 18th green on the Arnold Palmer course.

First Day Covers featured Des Smyth, former Irish Ryder Cup player, who was selected as one of the European team vice-captains in 2006.

▼ **The 12th**
An outline of the expansive 12th green on the newer Smurfit course protected by many sand traps. It is essential to get the tee shot close to the pin as three putting is frequent on what is reputed to be one of the largest individual greens you will encounter anywhere.

◄ **The 17th**
The high-rise teeing area for the 17th hole on the Ryder Cup course, called Mayfly Corner because of its proximity to the River Liffey, once famous for its salmon.

KILLARNEY
GOLF AND FISHING CLUB

Mahony's Point, Killarney, County Kerry

It is a compliment to Killarney Golf and Fishing Club, to give it its full and formal title, that any descriptive reference to it must be prefaced by acknowledgment of its beauty.

The tourism capital of Ireland is, the locals would have you believe: 'Heaven's own reflex — the end result of what the good Lord Almighty can do when He's in a good mood.' It is impossible to disagree.

Immortalised in song by the great Bing Crosby, Killarney's golf complex is surely without equal in terms of its photogenic qualities. It is located in the valley below the Macgillycuddy Reek mountain range, beside the lapping shores of the shimmering lakes and is particularly splendid when the rhododendrons are in bloom.

In golfing terms as well, Killarney also stands apart. It boasts three wonderful courses, the combined reputation of which is acknowledged everywhere. The dilemma is which one to choose.

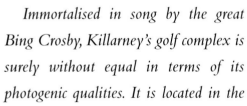

MAHONY'S POINT
YARDS
6,870
PAR
72
TYPE
Parkland

OLD KILLEEN
YARDS
7,121
PAR
71
TYPE
Parkland

LACKABANE
YARDS
7,051
PAR
71
TYPE
Parkland
LOCATION
2 miles/3.2 km west of Killarney
EMAIL
reservations@
killarney-golf.com
WEB
www.killarney-golf.com

Henry Longurst and Sir Guy Campbell were the co-designers of Mahony's Point.

The Killeen, designed by former club stalwart, the late Dr. Billy O'Sullivan in association with Eddie Hackett, run side by side with it around the lakes. Across the road is the newer Lackabane, designed by Donald Steel.

Pride of place has been awarded to the Old Killeen, as it is now referred to, as when the Irish Open championship was designated to the County Kerry resort in 1990 and 1991, it won the nomination, when the temptation was resisted to come up with a compromise of it and Mahony's Point.

Old Killeen, since handsomely upgraded with particular reference to its water features, won much adulation, although it seemed a shame that the famous 18th hole on the Mahony's Point course could not be used. Local folklore recalls a golfer slicing his ball into the lake from the tee where it hit and killed a rising trout, after which he allegedly waded into the water to retrieve the ball — and the fish!

◄◄ **Majestic setting**
Killarney Golf Club is set
beneath the majestic
Macgillycuddy Reeks and
Ireland's highest mountain,
Carrantuohil.

▲ **The 10th**
The renowned par three, 10th
hole on the Old Killeen course,
which is fronted by the lake
and with the scenic mountains
in background.

◀ **Lakeside breeze**
A westerly breeze stirs the lake on a bright, sunny day that shows off the course to its best.

◀ **The 18th - Mahony's Point**
A do-or-die climax without equal at one of the most scenic points of the old Mahony's Point course.
An inlet of the lake extends the near 200-yard length of the hole. It is carry all the way to reach the long but narrow strip of green where the lake shore laps the right hand flank and a series of pot bunkers mark the left hand side beneath the towering pines.
Club selection can be a dilemma, more so if the choppy waters are accompanied by a rising wind.
196 yards
Par 3

◀ **The 17th**
The testing 17th hole on Mahony's Point runs alongside the lake shoreline. And it's easy to be distracted by the view.

◀ **Heaven's reflex**
'Heaven's own reflex' is one of the poetic descriptions of the surroundings of Killarney. It's easy to see why.

Oasis ▷
A sylvan oasis at the heart of
the upgraded Old Killeen course.

▼ **The 18th**
One of the most fabled finishing
holes in golf: the classic lakeside
par three, 18th hole, a memorable
grand finale to the Mahony's Point
championship course.

Glories of Killarney

Killarney proudly markets itself as Ireland's tourism capital. Aside from golf, it is well served with amenities to suit all tastes. Boating and fishing on the famous lakes, mountain climbing on Ireland's highest range, and walking tours will satisfy the energetic tourist. Cultural and archivist interests are catered for in the magnificent Muckross House. A motor car museum and the annual Killarney race festival are other options.

▲▲ By Killarney's lakes
The backdrop to virtually every hole at Killarney is as magnificent as the next

▲ The 4th
A high-rise optional tee on the Killeen course's 4th hole.

LAHINCH
GOLF CLUB

Lahinch, County Clare

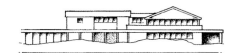

OLD COURSE
YARDS
6,950

PAR
72

CASTLE COURSE
YARDS
5,556

PAR
70

TYPE
Links

LOCATION
2 miles / 3.2 km
west of Ennistymon,
to Lahinch village.

TYPE
Links

EMAIL
info@lahinchgolfclub.com

WEB
www.lahinchgolfclub.com

Given that the links at Lahinch owe their legend principally to the craftsmanship of Old Tom Morris and Dr. Alister MacKenzie, the leading designers of the day, the noted contemporary golf architect, Martin Hawtree, can feel he completes a distinguished trio.

In respectful appreciation of what they inherited from Morris and MacKenzie back in the 19th and 20th centuries, the caring members of Lahinch presented Hawtree with the 21st century brief, to 'restore the links and incorporate modern design and construction techniques to ensure Lahinch keeps pace with golf trends and remains a test for the world's best, while continuing to be a pleasant links for the members and visitors alike.'

To Hawtree's credit, that vision has truly been satisfied. Today, an invigorated Lahinch unfolds after a painstaking four year project, with the remodelling of some fourteen holes, the introduction of two completely new ones, the elimination of the original par three 3rd and a new hole sequence.

The refurbishment enhances its reputation because nowhere in Ireland do you find the members and local villagers more consciously aware of the historical importance of golf, set by the Atlantic in the heart of the spectacularly beautiful West Clare countryside.

That special golfing character is further evidenced by the insistence that in face of change, the unique flavour of the infamous Klondyke and Dell holes should remain sacrosanct.

Set against modern architectural trends, these old-fashioned blind hand-me-downs are outdated. But it would surely be tantamount to sacrilege to have broken a tradition established by Tom Morris, endorsed by Alister MacKenzie and lovingly preserved down through the generations by the late Brud Slattery, for so long the proud custodian of the club's better virtues.

A harmless concession was the change in hole sequence – the Klondyke and Dell moving one hole

forward to become the 4th and 5th, caused by the elim-ination of the 3rd. *The par three 8th at 166 yards is a new hole in a previously idle dune, across a deep valley, to a green, sandwiched between more dunes.*

Coincidentally, the other new hole is also a par three. It replaces a previous but defunct one-shotter at the 11th. It is another beauty, tucked away in a most idyllic seaside spot on the shores of Liscannor Bay.

◀◀ The 3rd

The fabulous location of the green for the dramatic new 3rd hole overlooking Liscannor Bay. Your drive must rise over a 30-foot dune to high ground from where the green is glimpsed beyond a succession of humps, hollows and rough. The humbling 446 yards challenge also takes account of a deep bunker tucked into the left hand approach to the green.

▼ Savour the experience!

A perfect depiction of the components that mark the uniqueness of Lahinch; aglorious setting; a rich history; superb natural beauty and superlative topography.

▲ The 6th

Lahinch's powerful 6th hole, showing the trademark 'mine' in the foreground, over which the second shot must be aimed at a green lying against a breath-taking backdrop of the Atlantic.

▼ The 5th - The Dell - Old Course

No hole in golf is as famous as The Dell at Lahinch.
A throw-back to the original designer, Old Tom Morris, this is an unorthodox blind hole of great renown, outdated but lovingly preserved.
Look out for the white-washed stone on top of the sand hill straight in front of you and blocking your view of the green. The stone marks the line to the hole on the narrow green concealed behind.
154 yards
Par 3

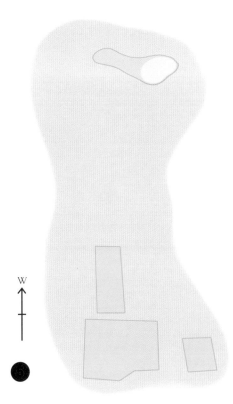

▲ O'Connor's castle

A reminder of times long past where a castle belonging to the
O'Connor clan – who often fought battles at Lahinch against
rival chieftains – still stands alongside the par three 6th hole
on the less forbidding and aptly named Castle course.

From times past

An image of the gracious old Golf Links Hotel, close by the terminus
of the fabled West Clare Railway line, which became immortalised in
song by Percy French, and where reports of the era tell of 'the golfers
partaking in the splendour of the hotel's hot and cold sea water baths
during their golfing sojourns'.

◄ **The 10th and 13th**
A wonderful vista looking
down over the 10th and
13th greens across the Old
Course and beyond to the
Inagh River and the Castle
Course.

MOUNT JULIET
GOLF CLUB

Thomastown, County Kilkenny

The acclamation from Tiger Woods that Mount Juliet presented 'perfect fairways … and the best greens we have putted on including the Majors' was powerful approval of the stature of Ireland's leading championship parkland golf course.

The classic course – selected venue for three Irish Opens, two American Express World championships and an equally absorbing head to head Shell Wonderful World of Golf contest between Fred Couples and Tom Watson – is the centrepiece of a new concept for golf in Ireland.

It was here, at the instigation of the visionary Dr. Tim Mahony, that luxury golf was unveiled for the first time in Ireland.

Built around an imposing 18th century mansion, which has been converted into a five star hotel managed under the Conrad flag, Mount Juliet also includes the Hunter's Yard clubhouse, offering the very best accommodation and dining. There is also the opportunity for fishing, clay

YARDS
7,264

PAR
72

LOCATION
Thomastown village

TYPE
Parkland

EMAIL
info@mountjuliet.ie

WEB
www.mountjuliet.com

River Nore at Kilkenny

target shooting, horse riding and walking many secluded trails.

The perceptive hand of Jack Nicklaus – aided by Jeff Howse who then conceived the adjoining and unique putting course – has converted the 1,500 acre estate into an acclaimed, custom built oasis, the merits of which are warmly endorsed by all.

Water abounds on this course, most notably on the back nine on what is unashamedly an American-type course and where lavishly contoured fairways and ornately sculptured bunkers blend happily with the many species of trees which have been planted.

The par three 3rd, up to 200 yards over water, is an early challenge – and a scary one. Water is again a factor at the 4th, and on the more difficult back nine, it features as a potential hazard at the 11th, 13th and on either side of the lake that bisects the powerful finishing 17th and 18th holes.

◄◄ **Nicklaus legacy**
The golfing experience of a lifetime.
A Jack Nicklaus designed course set in a
wonderfully mature parkland estate.

▶ **The 10th**
An abundance of sand
traps emphasise the
brilliant design and
challenge of the split
fairway 10th hole.

▼ **The 2nd**
The second green is well guarded by a
gracefully designed, and superbly
maintained bunker.

▲ **The 13th**

If ever a hole merited its status
as Index 1, Mount Juliet's
signature 13th truly has the
capacity to be nominated the
most difficult hole on the
course.

Dropping steeply downhill, it is
imperative to get a good and
accurate drive away.

Otherwise the chance to go for
the green is diluted by the
prospect of a watery grave in
the lake which expands all too
invitingly to the front of the
green.

433 yards
Par 4

◄ **The 18th**

An outstanding finishing
hole with the lake in play
for its entire length. The
famous 18th calls for two
long and accurate shots
to reach the green.

▼ **Tranquility**
A peaceful setting within Ireland's largest
walled estate of 1,500 acres.

Sand sculpture ▶
Ornately sculptured bunkers
are a feature element of
every hole on Mount Juliet.

▼ **The 3rd**
Water is the principal element of consideration when selecting a club at the widely acclaimed 'white knuckle' par three, 3rd hole.

Fulsome praise

The most enduring and telling testaments of the merits of Mount Juliet are contained in the sentiments of the world stars who have played there. Phil Mickelson heaped fulsome praise when he said he could 'hardly believe the place' and that 'it was a fantastic venue', while fellow US tour colleague Scott McCarron was so consumed with what he discovered that he declared Mount Juliet as a 'Must See' destination for all tourists heading to Ireland.

OLD HEAD
GOLF LINKS

Kinsale, County Cork

It is difficult to argue as you behold the sight of the Old Head golf links that is not indeed the most spectacular golf course you will ever encounter.

Perched atop an Atlantic promontory on the southern tip of Ireland, hundreds of feet above dramatic cliff faces, your senses are heightened by the crashing roar of the ocean waves beneath.

'This stunning setting creates the potential to become the eighth wonder of the world in golfing terms' enthused the late Joe Carr, one of Ireland's greatest golfing heroes. Well might he praise a course which he conceived in committee with such renowned design experts as Ron Kirby, Patrick Merrigan and Eddie Hackett.

The Old Head at Kinsale is a national monument. Its history is traceable to several centuries before Christ. It is included in the Inventory of Outstanding Landscapes in Ireland and is a place of outstanding historical, archaeological and scientific interest.

YARDS
7,215

PAR
72

LOCATION
From Kinsale take route
R 600/R640

TYPE
Links

EMAIL
info@oldheadgolf.ie

WEB
www.oldheadgolflinks.com

Shop fronts in Kinsale

Locals would have you believe that some remains of human settlement are still to be found, visible as small circles of stone which are thought to be the remnants of huts dating to the Ice Age. Legend has it that the Celtic tribe Erin, Ireland's first settlers, lit fires as navigational assistance to seafarers.

While today the Old Head is a place of pilgrimage for golfers, its virtue is enhanced by its unique location close by the ancient harbour town of Kinsale, also known as the Gourmet Capital of Ireland.

Exposed as it is on an expansive diamond of land jutting powerfully into the Atlantic, the Old Head is not for the faint hearted. Nine of its holes are perched, precariously at times, along the rugged cliff faces and all eighteen of its holes command stunning views of the surrounding sea.

The vagaries of the weather more often determine your fate, although you need not baulk as the forgiving design team had the forethought to provide a wide selection of less fearsome tee options. Don't let your vanity spoil the experience.

Either way, the challenge is not lessened on this par 72 moonscape, whose championship length stretches to 7,215 yards – plus the wind factor! There the five par 5s, five par 3s and eight par 4s configured to make the most of the breath-taking 360 degree vistas.

The most spectacular golf course on the planet?

The 8th ▶

The view from the green at the 8th hole which is known, for good reason as God's acre!

◀◀ Dramatic landscape
The quite stunning setting of Old Head is dramatically seen here, perched atop an Atlantic promontory on the southern tip of Ireland.

▼ Lighthouse sentinel
The lighthouse at the southern most tip of the course stands sentinel over an extraordinary golfing location as well as a place of historical, archaeological and scientific interest.

◀ **The 12th**
Proceed with caution as the narrowing fairway on the intimidating 12th hole runs perilously close to the steep cliff face above the Atlantic.

▼ **The 7th - Legal Eagle**
When seven of the world's leading golfers, including Tiger Woods, Mark O'Meara, David Duval and Lee Janzen, played this hole in preparation for a British Open championship: only one matched par! This fascinating creation mirrors much of the Old Head's challenge, as its spectacular setting starkly presents the intimidating sight and sound of the adjacent Atlantic. With water to one side and the out-of-bounds roadway to the other, there seems no let-off. Even the 'bail out' option to the left of the green offers little solace insofar as the chip shot is to a putting surface running onwards and onwards, seemingly the length of the entire coastline.
188 yards
Index 8
Par 3

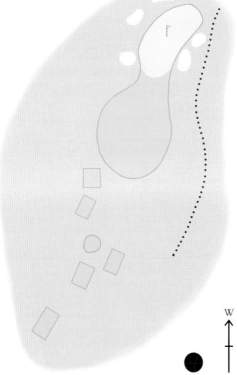

W

Seal a deal

Part of the ancient history of the area is the Stone of Accord or Wedding Stone which has been adopted as the logo of Old Head and stands by the starter's hut. The rounded limestone rock was used for centuries to symbolically 'seal a deal' by participants placing their fingers through either side of the small hole cut in the top of the stone.

▲ **Eighth Wonder**
Joe Carr, one of the design team of the course saw the Old Head as the Eighth Wonder of the World in golfing terms.

◄ The 16th
A tight and thrilling par three, the 16th as seen from behind its green which is jealously protected by two pot bunkers to the left.

▼ Awesome setting
The weather-beaten landscape from which the Old Head was crafted to become one of the most dramatically sited courses in the world.

PGA National Ireland
Golf Course

Palmerstown House, Johnstown, County Kildare

For one who professes not to play golf, the businessman Jim Mansfield certainly has a perceptive eye for the game's potential.

His unearthing of Palmerstown House, a lush and imperial 800-acre estate and one time stud farm of international repute, has truly underlined the entrepreneur's facility to identify and develop a golfing opportunity.

What strikes one immediately about the grandly named PGA National Ireland is its potential to become one of the most prized golfing locations in the country, a mere 30 minutes from bustling downtown Dublin city, yet muffled from the madding crowd by ancient forests of mature woodlands.

'It was probably one of the easiest assignments I had to do', reflects designer Christy O'Connor Jnr, in respect of a setting which nature had so generously bestowed for conversion to a golfing sanctuary.

The end product is a quite stunning resource, idyllically at peace in a majestic setting where each hole

PGA NATIONAL Ireland

YARDS
7,419

PAR
72

LOCATION
30 miles south of Dublin on N7, heading for Naas

TYPE
Parkland

EMAIL
pganational@
palmerstownhouse.com

WEB
www.palmerstownhouse.com

The Curragh race course at dawn.

boasts its own individual attraction and where the entire course equals the best that you will encounter.

The lustre of the development is heightened by the decision of the Professional Golfers Association to name it PGA National Ireland and also utilise the amenity as its official Irish headquarters.

This is a ground-breaking gesture within Ireland, equalled only by the PGA National at The Belfry in England, celebrated home to so many great Ryder Cup moments, and the PGA Centenary course at revered Gleneagles, in Scotland.

A further measure of this extraordinary retreat is that its rich pasturelands once provided the compliant setting for a world-famous horse-racing yard and stud farm. Now it is destined to also gain golfing acclaim.

Where the design concept really captures the imagination is in its rich diversity. O'Connor Jnr's trade-mark, architectural far-sightedness is readily to hand, as shown in the contouring of sweeping fairways, the wily placement of bunkering and the

◀ **The 3rd**
The charming
characteristics of each
individual hole are
beautifully captured
across the tranquil
lake leading
to the 3rd green.

103

forceful usage of water, the latter as an aesthetic feature on the one hand or as a destructive defence tool on the other.

Such is the variety, there is lots of merit from which to choose. O'Connor's own preference is for the 7th, a winding Par 4 of 427 yards.

It is presented as a tormenting conundrum, initially requiring a more offensive drive to flirt with the left hand bunkers, the payback being the reward of a clearer vision of the green. Regardless, the challenge is unrelenting as the brief now is not merely to hit the green, but to do so with an accuracy that finds the optimum spot on any one of three levels where the green keeper Satan could, in devilish mood, cut the hole in the middle of any one of a number of slopes and contours.

The designer's classical philosophy is also evidenced at the Par 4, 428 yards 4th hole. It is an absolute gem. The distinctive boathouse roof provides a line off the tee, from where only a cracking drive will offer a genuine chance of traversing the lake to the island green. Anything less and you feel mystified; foolhardy to take on the water but cowardly not to accept the challenge. Little wonder the locals describe it as awe-inspiring.

You might well nominate any of the holes as a favourite, such is their impact. The four par 5s for example are truly outstanding creations and significantly Indexed 1 to 4. Or, you might opt for the Par 4, 18th of 448 yards, where water hogs the left-hand flank and bunkers guard the long and sloping green, nestling under the balcony of the imposing clubhouse.

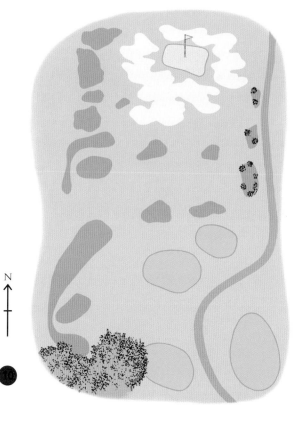

The 10th
Stunning in its design and set to become one of the most photographed holes in Irish golf, this magnificent hole excels in its detail. The green is set in splendid isolation and is surrounded by menacing bunkers. The key is club selection, allied to conviction of its execution. Hold tight!
Par 3
178 yards

N

▲ **Practice greens**
Forewarned is forearmed: the exotically located choice of four practice putting greens set amidst the colourful flora.

◄ Another glimpse of the scenic layout.

◄ **7th hole**
'Christy's Fun Green' as dedicated by course architect, Christy O'Connor Jnr.

Christy O'Connor Jnr

Christy O'Connor Jnr, left, the golfer, is best known for the two-iron shot he hit over the water and onto the green at the Belfry's 18th hole to help clinch the 1989 Ryder Cup; as a course designer, his legend may well be the creation of the superb Palmerstown House course.

As he said of his design:
'I was inspired by being presented with what has to be one of the best sites in the world and which reminded me of going through the gates at Augusta National ... up Magnolia Lane ... and into the US Masters Tournament'.

▲ **Ideal location**
Sunset on a serene location only thirty minutes 30 minutes from Dublin city yet protected from urban bustle by old forests of mature woodlands.

◄◄ **10th hole**
Stately Palmerstown House was once home to such notables as the 7th Earl of Mayo and the eminent William Bullitt, former American Ambassador to Paris and Moscow.

PORTMARNOCK
GOLF CLUB

Portmarnock, County Dublin

Reverentially regarded as the golfing equivalent of a national heirloom, Portmarnock Golf Club stands sentinel on a rugged peninsula jutting out into the Irish Sea. It is regarded as the premier club in the Republic of Ireland.

The evolution and popularity of the game can trace its roots to the north County Dublin club. Were it not for the generosity of its members back in the late 1920s, the Irish Open Championship might never have been instituted. They dug deep into their pockets to ensure that Irish golf could be showcased.

It is also acknowledged that the success of the 1959 Dunlop Masters, followed by the World (then named Canada) Cup in 1960, and won by the charismatic Sam Snead and the up and coming Arnold Palmer were the catalyst for the ensuing growth of interest in golf, not only in Ireland but worldwide.

Subsequent stagings of the Irish Open at Portmarnock in the 1970s and 80s attracted some

YARDS
7,362

PAR
72

LOCATION
10 miles/16 km
north-east of Dublin City
to Portmarnock village

TYPE
Links

EMAIL
portmarnockgolfclub.ie

WEB
www.portmarnockgolfclub.ie

Hill of Howth

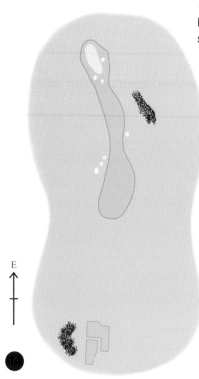

◄ The 14th
Even if modern technology serves to dilute the threat of a hole measuring just over 400 yards, this classical right-to-left design has surrendered little of its notoriety.

Taking a line on the distant landmark of Ireland's Eye, the premium is on a right hand tee shot, so as to avoid rough terrain on the left, as well as some bunkers.

Then a high, well-struck approach is the order, being careful to avoid some nasty traps by the narrow greenside.

411 yards
Par 4

E
↑

◄◄ The 6th
Portmarnock's formidable par five, 6th hole, at 603 yards one of the most critical challenges on the links.

of the world's greatest players and further added to the popularity of the game.

A major clubhouse re-development, which retains the character of the older building, enhances even further the 27 hole links.

The much-loved Harry Bradshaw, who was resident professional at the club for almost forty years, always affectionately drew attention to his favourite 5th hole, preferably played off the lower tee. Tom Watson wondered aloud as to why the Open Championship itself wasn't played there.

Ben Crenshaw was so captivated by the short 15th that he longed to take it back home to the USA, and for Bobby Locke the par four 14th was one of the greatest holes in the world.

There are few who have matched par on all final three holes especially if the prevailing south west wind is blowing.

There are many who believe that Ryder Cup 2006 should in fact have been allocated to Portmarnock — the spiritual home of Irish golf.

◄ The 9th
Picture postcard setting for the 9th green on the Blue Nine – an addition to the championship course and one which contains many outstanding holes of its own.

▲ **The 15th**
One of Portmarnock's most famous holes is the par three, 15th, 190 yards off the back tee – and dubbed by its designer as 'my revenge on posterity'. It is played from an eye-catching point parallel to the Irish Sea, which can provide an additional test when the wind is from the east.

▲ The 18th
The Championship 18th hole looking towards the raised green to the refurbished clubhouse beyond, where the distinguishing character of the previous building has been affectionately preserved.

The 12th ▶
Even a tee shot to the heart of the green will not guarantee a par three on this deceptively difficult hole.

A watery journey

Access to Portmarnock was originally by horse and trap at low tide or by rowing boat across the inlet from the mainland at Baldoyle.

A ship's bell was tolled each evening to signal the departure of the last means of transport.

To this day, it hangs on the clubhouse gable wall and is one of the many memorabilia preserved in the superb clubhouse.

▲▲ **The 4th**
A view from behind the restful 4th green set against the backdrop of Howth Head.

▲ **Quintessential**
A sanctuary of bracken, colourful gorse, rolling dune, natural bunkers; the essence of the links at Portmarnock, the Republic of Ireland's premier course.

PORTMARNOCK HOTEL
AND GOLF LINKS

Portmarnock, County Dublin

A shoulder-to-shoulder neighbour to the more esteemed Portmarnock Golf Club and destined to live in that shadow, the new Portmarnock Hotel and Golf Links nonetheless has its own outstanding qualities.

The discovery and adaptation of its pure linksland, in conjunction with the provision of an on-site hotel facility, is a tribute to those who conceived this new adornment to the eastern seaboard. Without question, it has successfully become a core element of the new golfing face of Ireland.

The choice of Ryder Cup star Bernhard Langer as its designer, in association with Stan Eby, has given to the course what has rightly been described as 'a design and layout that is notable for the fact that it manages the quite uncanny blend of the traditional perspective with all that is best in modern architectural trends.'

While the sting is in the tail, there is an eerie foreboding to start with. The 1st hole adjoins the

YARDS
6,880

PAR
71

LOCATION
10 miles / 16 km north of
Dublin city to Malahide

TYPE
Links

EMAIL
mcassidy@portmarnock.com

WEB
www.portmarnock.com

Ireland's Eye

graveyard home of Saint Marnock, after whom the local area and complex is named. That touch of Christian heritage quite often evokes the idea that the good Lord himself intended this particular tract of land for conversion to golf. He would have appreciated the result.

Indeed local tradition has it that the land upon which the links is built, which was once the home of the famous Jameson whiskey family, was in fact one of Ireland's earlier courses when developed for the family's private pleasure.

The opening holes are packaged as a more forgiving entrée, as, truth to tell, once the configuration makes it way towards the shore, the vagaries of links golf unfurl, frequently with a vengeance, especially if the Irish Sea is rough.

In that event, it quickly dawns on the unsuspecting player that early missed opportunities come home to roost as the sequence of six 4s and two par threes, starting at the Index 1, 11th offer little forgiveness.

◄◄ The 18th ►

The elegant outline of the splendid
hotel and clubhouse is a welcoming
backdrop to a powerful climax.
However, before savouring its
delights there is some tough
navigation, as the drive is a tight
one from amidst the dunes.
The recommended line is the left-
hand side from where your reward
should be a mid-iron approach to a
green located in a natural
amphitheatre. The ample defence of
bunkers left and right await to
ensnare those who cannot match the
links' final challenge to stamina and
nerve.

448 yards
Par 4

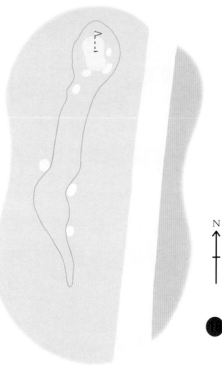

N

▲ Superb facilities
Luxury facilities form an imposing
and elegant backdrop to the superb
Portmarnock Hotel and Golf Links on
the coast of north County Dublin

◄ Amid the dunes
Nestled amid the dunes and
alongside the famous strand
from which two pioneering trans-
Atlantic flights took off in the
early 1930s.

▼ Classic location
'There are very few locations in Europe that could
have allowed me the opportunity and landscape to
design such a classic championship links. I hope all
those who play it discover its magic and challenging
beauty', said course designer Bernhard Langer.

POWERSCOURT

GOLF CLUB

Powerscourt Estate, Enniskerry, County Wicklow

Given that Powerscourt has one of the most celebrated landscape settings of all 18th century country houses and estates, it followed quite naturally that it would lend itself to the development of a golf course.

So good was the conversion, that having built one course to the design concepts of former British amateur champion, Peter McEvoy, a second was then added and designed by the Scot, David McKay Kidd.

A common denominator between the East and West courses is that they share some of the finest scenery in County Wicklow, from the rugged uplands of the Wicklow Mountains to the superb vista of the Big Sugarloaf.

A measure of the quality of the East course is that within two years of opening, it was chosen as the venue for the Irish PGA National Championship. Three years later, it hosted the AIB Irish Seniors Open.

POWERSCOURT
GOLF CLUB

EAST COURSE

YARDS
7,063

PAR
72

WEST COURSE

YARDS
6,987

PAR
72

LOCATION
12 miles/19 km south of Dublin on N 11 to Enniskerry village

EMAIL
golfclub@powerscourt.ie

WEB
www.powerscourt.ie/golfclub

Within its picturesque landscape, there is a host of outstanding holes whose eccentric moods can be further experienced if the wind is from the east.

Harsh, undulating greens are commonplace and quickly focus the mind, although the surrounding landscape is rich compensation if things go wrong.

It is essential on the East course to maintain concentration and tempo. The climax has the potential to wreck your card. From the short 16th onwards, you truly walk the Powerscourt gauntlet.

On the newer West course, your fate may be determined a little earlier. The 4th, a par four is generally regarded as the toughest. The drive is over a ravine and the onus on accuracy is emphasised by the doom threatened by the corner of the dog-leg, which brings out of bounds sharply into the frame.

On the homeward journey, one of the hardest holes is likely to be the dog-leg par five, 16th. It is imperative to produce your best drive in order to carry a fairway bunker. A cross-bunker means your next decision is to lay up short - or go for glory!

▲ **The 16th**
The signature 16th hole on the newer West course is dominated the Big Sugarloaf.

◄◄ **Mature setting**
Powerscourt's wonderfully mature setting amidst some of the finest scenery in County Wicklow, known as the Garden of Ireland.

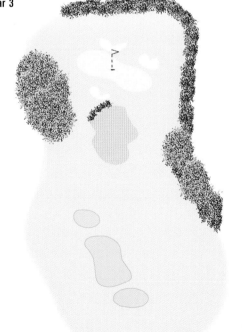

▲ **The 16th**
A well-positioned bunker defence increases the challenge in reaching the 16th green on the West course.

▼ **The 16th - East course**
A delightful par three, of which it is said that the 12th at Augusta National may have been on designer McEvoy's mind when he fashioned this hole at such a critical point in the round. Mischievousness may have had the heavier hand, given the obstacles of lake, bunkers, trees and a relatively small, angled green.
The putting surface is set in a protective cul-de-sac of pine trees and even if the lake fronting the green is safely crossed, it is imperative to land with precision on the sloping surface.
145 yards
Par 3

The 4th ▶
Do not take a risk on the East's 4th hole where over aggression might lead to an out of bounds on the right and rough on a steep bank to the left. Accuracy is more important than length.

W

RATHSALLAGH HOUSE

GOLF AND COUNTRY CLUB

Dunlavin, County Wicklow

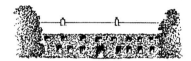

Augusta without the azalea was an intuitive if somewhat overstated emotion on a first visit to this magnificent retreat in the heart of County Wicklow.

Playing under a clear blue sky, in warm sunshine and to the calming backdrop of brooks and birdsong, it was the complete golfing experience in a quite spectacular setting amidst the sylvan estate, housing the Rathsallagh House Golf and Country Club.

Set in 250-odd acres, this dramatic course can justifiably be classified as championship quality. Certainly it is as good a parkland layout as you will find in Ireland.

Furthermore, the enticing course is complemented by an outstanding clubhouse designed so that its strategic lofty positioning affords wide views of many holes, especially the telling 9th, 10th and 18th.

The complex also includes a golf academy with excellent facilities such as pitch and putt, tutorial practice range and high-tech computer coaching and teaching aids.

YARDS
6,885

PAR
72

LOCATION
Off N7 1 mile/1.5 km
south of Dunlavin village

TYPE
Parkland

EMAIL
info@rathsallagh.com

WEB
www.rathsallagh.com

River Glenealo

You must salute the design team of Christy O'Connor Jnr and Peter McEvoy for the manner in which they wove a pattern through the dense foliage between the shimmering lakes and meandering streams and presented such a challenging mix of holes.

Rathsallagh justifiably prides itself on its extremely high maintenance standards, which enable play throughout the year. Notable features are the large,

contoured greens designed to USGA specifications. They provide magnificently true putting surfaces and, be forewarned, frequently of a speed not normally experienced on most other parkland courses.

The appeal of the greens and bunker designs blend beautifully into the majestic setting. There are many feature holes, not least in the vicinity of the clubhouse from where, of course, you will be conscious of preying and critical eyes!

The 9th ▶
The strategically positioned and distinctive clubhouse commands fine views of many of the holes, including the 9th green.

◀◀ Rainbow's end
A crock of gold at the end of the rainbow, perhaps? A passing rain shower provides a dramatic frame for the magnificent setting of Rathsallagh.

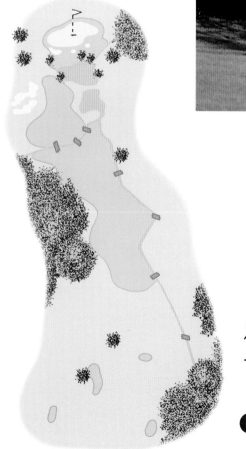

The 6th ▶
Water hogs the length of the right hand side, culminating in an expansive lake for the challenging last passage leading to the green.
Trees left place further pressure on the drive and even if that test is accomplished, boldly going for the green in two is obviously a high risk gamble.
More prudently you might settle for a three-shot strategy and the better prospect of a trophy par.
502 yards
Par 5

▲ Picture setting
The rolling parkland, mature foliage, lakes and streams of Rathsallagh provide a particularly picturesque setting for golf.

S

The 4th ▶
Water and sand combine to make the delightful par three, 4th hole a test of nerves and accuracy.

◄ **Heirloom**
History speaks from every stone of
Rathsallagh Country House, which dates
from 1798 and was originally converted
from Queen Anne stables.

ROYAL COUNTY DOWN

Newcastle, County Down

Whatever occurs at animated 19th hole debates on the merits, or otherwise of golf courses, you will get unanimity about one thing: Royal County Down is above reproach. It is universally held to be one of the world's finest golf destinations.

Where the Mountains of Mourne sweep down to the sea lies the lovely links beside the town of

Newcastle, characteristically set against its time-honoured image of the golden expanse of Dundrum Bay, the distinctive red brick silhouette of the Slieve Donard Hotel and onwards to the varying hues of the mountains.

The second oldest club in Northern Ireland, preceeded only by Royal Belfast is blessed by its architectural lineage. It was essentially laid out by the wily eye of immortal Old Tom Morris; further revisions were by the hands of Vardon and Colt. Little wonder it has endured as one of golf's truly classic links.

YARDS
7,181

PAR
71

LOCATION
30 miles/48 km south
of Belfast, to Newcastle

TYPE
Links

EMAIL
royalcountydown.org

WEB
www.royalcountydown.org

Dundrum Bay

Not everybody favours the club's strict jacket-and-tie policy. Yet perversely, this austere attitude somehow adds to its distinctiveness and old-fashioned charm.

By the same token there is forgiveness about the half dozen or so blind shots that the course throws up. The compensation is that golf at Royal County Down is an experience that simply sets it apart. Each hole, set in that distinctive heather-strewn landscape, provides ample evidence.

Take, for example, the storied 9th (see page 128). You might express similar sentiments of the par three 4th, which offers such wonderful views from the elevated tee; or the special character of the tough 13th; the teasing, short par four, 16th. And certainly of the absorbing finishing par five 18th, where you are required to navigate your safe passage home around 24 bunkers!

'Exhilarating, even without a club in your hand' is said of a links where history records that the brief presented to Old Tom Morris was to 'lay out a links at a cost not to exceed four guineas'!

◀◀ **Famous setting**
The superb setting of the lovely Royal County Down links with its distinctive clubhouse, at the foot of the Mourne Mountains is one of the most photographod viowc in golf.

▼ **Links elements**
Sand dunes and gorse in abundance provide the classic elements of links golf.

▲ **The 9th**
A hole which exhilarates and terrifies.
A long and elevated blind tee shot, must clear the brow of the 'viewing' hill onto the fairway 80 feet below. More brawn is again required as you hit into the scenic backdrop of the hotel, townland and mountain range, all the while conscious to avoid those two infamous bunkers, 50 yards short of the green.
486 yards
Par 4

The 13th ▶
The par four, 444 yard, 13th hole is one of the toughest on the links, where the green forms its own amphitheatre to provide a unique atmosphere surrounded by colourful gorse.

▲ **The 5th**
Be forewarned: anything moving right of the white
stone at which a blind tee shot must be aimed will
catch the tangled and plentiful heather along the
right hand side of the 5th fairway.

ROYAL DUBLIN

GOLF CLUB

Dollymount, Dublin 3

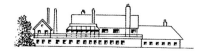

Royal Dublin is the longest established club in Dublin, dating to 1892. It is also distinguished by being sited within the boundaries of a wildlife preserve, just fifteen minutes bus ride from the capital city. It is said to be the first club in Ireland to have had an eighteen-hole course and furthermore, the links partly owes its existence to the celebrated Captain William Bligh of Bounty seafaring fame.

It seems that Captain Bligh was invited, around the early 1800s, to make sugges-tions on how best to provide safe shipping up the River Liffey into the city. His influ-ences were such that the Bull Wall causeway was erected and the sandbank which subsequently formed ultimately yielded the rich crop of fescue grasses that provide the ideal terrain for a golf links.

At the outbreak of World War One, the links was occupied by the military for use as an artillery range and was returned some years later in a very dilapidated state. The compensation paid was used to engage the noted architect Harold Colt to create

YARDS
7,142

PAR
72

LOCATION
3 miles/5 km north east
of Dublin city. To Bull Wall
(Dollymount)

TYPE
Links

EMAIL
info@theroyaldublin
golfclub.ie

WEB
www.theroyaldublin
golfclub.com

Customs House, Dublin

the re-design. On its flat terrain and with its distinctive old traditional out-and-back concept, it is often said that there is a resemblance to St. Andrews, by whose influence Colt was inspired.

So as to maintain its top status, the club commissioned Martin Hawtree, one of the leading contemporary designers, to complement Colt's work with some updating. To his credit, the course that captured international acclaim in the mid 1980s when Seve Ballesteros (twice) and Bernhard Langer won memorable Irish Open championships, has now taken on a significant new dimension.

Another milestone was the first competitive appearances in Ireland by Jack Nicklaus when he played Seve Ballesteros in the 1985 Toyota Challenge of Champions. The Golden Bear highlighted the variety of the par threes as a feature he would remember. Ballesteros paid homage to the final three holes, perhaps in salute of Christy O'Connor Snr, for whom he had great admiration, and of O'Connor's once covering the stretch in eagle-birdie-eagle to snatch a famous tournament win.

◀◀ The Garden
Viewed from the clubhouse verandah, the 18th green, Royal Dublin's much celebrated finishing hole.

▼ Lordly
Royal Dublin's distinctive clubhouse lords above the 18th green and fairway at the illustrious Garden Hole whose difficulty is illustrated by the outline of the waterway which marks the out of bounds running from tee to green.

▶ The 18th
Royal Dublin's most celebrated hole – known as The Garden – is a sharp left to right dog-leg and an enthralling hole to finish a round. First obstacle is to get away as long a drive as possible; avoiding a bunker about 220 yards up the left. The hazard running the right hand length of the fairway must also be steered clear of, before weighing up the prospect of the 'glory' shot across the out-of-bounds Garden, or the safer three-shot strategy to the corner of the dog leg. You'll regret not going for broke!

475 yards
Par 4

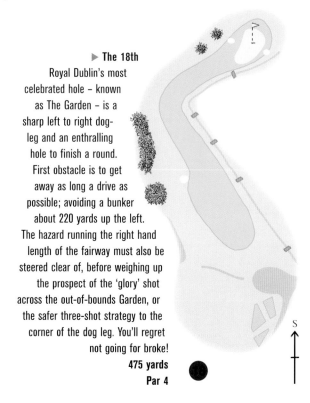

▲ The 8th
The par five, 8th running out to the extreme northern end of the links has the potential to yield a birdie for the longer hitters, although cleverly placed fairway and greenside bunkers can upset the best laid plans.

◄ The 6th
The long par three, 6th hole known as 'The Pot', is well-bunkered on the right hand side of the green. Also take account of the lateral water hazard running left from the tee to within 30 yards or so of the putting surface.

ROYAL PORTRUSH

GOLF CLUB

Portrush, County Antrim

In every discussion on great golf courses of the world, you will inevitably hear the claims of Royal Portrush being put forward.

One of the oldest clubs in Ireland – founded in 1888 – it is famous not only for its magnificent links, but also for the fact that it is synonymous with so many historical events.

The most remembered, of course, is that the lovely course within a drive and pitch of the busy seaside holiday resort of Portrush, hosted the only British Open championship ever staged outside mainland Britain, when the extrovert Max Faulkner won the 1951 title with a score of four under par 285.

Another notable link between Portrush and the Open championship is that Fred Daly, Ireland's only winner in 1947, hails from the area and learned to play his golf on the Dunluce course.

It should be noted that the unique setting also takes account of the lesser known, though very meritorious Valley course, and that both are

DUNLUCE

YARDS
6,845

PAR
72

VALLEY

YARDS
6,304

PAR
70

LOCATION
1 mile/1.6 km east
of Portrush

TYPE
Links

EMAIL
info@royalportrush
golfclub.com

WEB
www.royalportrush
golfclub.com

within easy reach of other great courses at Castlerock and Portstewart. The necklace forms a paradise of links courses.

The esteem with which Royal Portrush is held was demonstrated when one winter the ravages of the sea wreaked havoc on its exposed boundaries, and almost washed away the 5th hole. There was a universal response when the legendary Joe Carr pleaded its case. 'These links are one of the great heritages of golf,' he said. 'At any cost, they must be preserved for future generations of golfers'. The response was immediate.

The character of Dunluce is further emphasised by the par five 10th, the infamous par three 14th aptly named 'Calamity Corner' and the par five, 17th where you must resist the temptations of a formidable bunker, known locally as 'Big Nellie.'

For the more faint-hearted, the adjoining Valley links is an excellent alternative and used each year as a qualifying course for the North of Ireland amateur championship.

◄◄ **By golden sand**
Royal Portrush is laid out on a magnificent stretch of golden sand on the one side and the Antrim coast road leading out to the famous Giant's Causeway on the other.

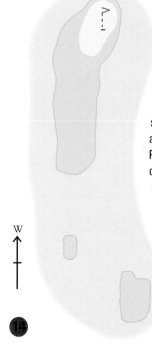

W

 The 14th
Named 'Calamity Corner', and aptly so, this is one of the most talked about golf holes in the game. Perched on a cliff edge, it's a full carry of 210 yards off the back stake across a chasm that falls away to the adjoining lower Valley course. Those who do not feel equipped for the challenge may instead aim for Bobby Locke's Hollow, a reprieving bale-out area to the left front corner of the green.
210 yards
Par 3

▲ **The 6th**
The 6th hole, named in honour of designer Harry Colt, early golf's architectural genius, and whose vision at Royal Portrush has made the links a place of golfing pilgrimage.

Fred Daly's
Fred Daly's hole, named in honour of Ireland's only winner of the British Open championship in 1947, and who learned his golf on the Portrush links. It has the most difficult tee shot on the links where the premium is on a long and accurate drive down the right so as to avoid a big bunker on the left hand line.

▼ The 2nd

Giant's Grave, the 2nd hole, a 505 yards par five where bunkers on the right are in play from the drive and where three more sand traps are devilishly placed close to the green. Even the longest hitters will have a decision to make before summoning the courage to take on the green in two shots.

▲ Three in one

The unique Royal Portrush complex, just a drive and a pitch shot from thefamous holiday sea-side town, is a well endowed golf facility of three courses: No.1, or Dunluce, on the higher and more open ground; the less challenging though greatly appealing No.2 Valley course below and the nine-hole pitch and putt course, called The Skerries.

The 7th ▶

Watch out for the strategically placed bunkers on the 7th hole, generally regarded as one of the best par fours to be found anywhere.

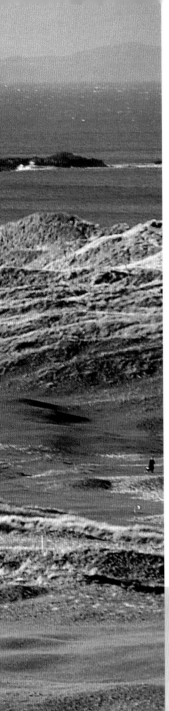

Uniquely Royal Portrush

Founded in 1888 and granted the Royal prefix seven years later when the Prince of Wales (later King Edward VII) was invited to become a patron, Royal Portrush holds a special place in the history of golf in Ireland. Many of the most notable historic milestones in the game are associated with the club, highlighted in modern times by the staging in 1951 of the only British Open championship ever held in Ireland and won by Max Faulkner.

▼ The 5th
The famous and much photographed 5th hole, offers great views of the White Rocks (after which the hole is named) and Giant's Causeway beyond. It is a much loved and chronicled hole and quite daunting during stormy weather in winter.

SLIEVE RUSSELL HOTEL
GOLF AND COUNTRY CLUB

Ballyconnell, County Cavan

The shrewd combination of luxury resort hotels with high quality golfing facilities, is a feature of the new commercial backbone of Ireland's changed golfing image.

A particularly good example of this may be found in Co. Cavan at Slieve Russell which embraces a luxury hotel, leisure and conference centre and a superb golf and country club.

Considering that the area does not have any golfing tradition, the business entrepreneur Sean Quinn has found a niche and developed a brand name that exemplifies all that is good in the modern golfing environment.

The previously unknown drumlin valley of west Cavan presented course architect Patrick Merrigan with a free hand – and, in character with a man who has made a significant architectural contribution to the Irish golfing scene, he duly created a masterpiece when he designed this outstanding course.

YARDS
7,053

PAR
72

LOCATION
2 miles north of
Ballyconnell on N3

TYPE
Parkland

EMAIL
slieve-reservations
@quinn-hotels.com

WEB
www.quinnhotels.com

Cross roads, County Cavan

A clue to what developed can be gauged by the titles subsequently allotted to some of the holes: 'Heron Haunt', 'Risky Rud', 'Watergate' and the 'Mourning Pond'- that latter description being self-explanatory!

A delightful blend of par threes, fours and fives underlines Merrigan's rather mischievous intent to exact a full dividend from the insertion of two large lakes which lie at the centre of this marvellous creation.

Little wonder that Slieve Russell has played host to a variety of important professional events, notably the Irish PGA championship and the North West of Ireland Open on the European Tour calendar.

The opinion of Christy O'Connor Snr stands as complimentary endorsement of what has been achieved at the Slieve Russell Golf and Country Club.

'One of my principal criteria in judging a golf course is that you get pleasure from it each time you play… and the more I play here, the more I want to come back'.

◄◄ **View from above**
A view from the air shows how architect Patrick Merrigan crafted his masterpiece course at Slieve Russell into the beautiful drumlin landscape of County Cavan.

▲ **Water, water everywhere**
Slieve Russell has fifty acres of lakes, many of them on the extraordinary back nine where the 11th, 12th, 13th and 16th are memorable features.

Slieve Russell Hotel ▶
The luxury hotel has numerous facilities that enhance the splendid course.

▲ The 11th
The thought provoking par three 11th, known as' Heron Haunt', which is a full blown 193 yards off the back tee and where you run the gauntlet of a lake and four shielding bunkers.

▶ The 13th
A double dog-leg of great length flanked for every yard by water. Off the back tee, it's 236 yards to carry the corner by the lake. Still, there is no let up while negotiating a narrow fairway. Finally, a sharp dog leg left across the water again. It is something of an achievement to stay dry throughout!
529 yards
Par 5

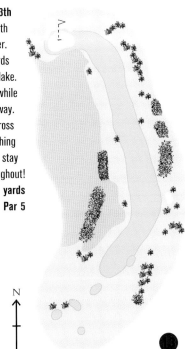

◀ Parkland course
The rolling landscape of County Cavan has been used skilfully to present one of Ireland's finest new parkland courses, which gets its name from a local beauty spot, known as Slieve Rushen.

TRALEE
GOLF CLUB

Barrow, County Kerry

The romantic success story of Tralee golf club can be compared, in a golfing sense, to the equivalent of winning the lottery.

Three times since the club was founded, in 1896, it had changed home to sites around the town, only each time to be plagued by higher than average rainfall which curtailed meaningful play. Then they discovered the site for a potential fourth home at Barrow, on the outskirts of town. The rest, as we say, is history.

Appraising his first ever golf course design in Europe, the great Arnold Palmer mused: 'We have one of the world's great links here. I designed the front nine, but surely God provided the rest!'

You can appreciate his veneration when you take account of the fact that the location overlooks stunning Banna Strand, portrayed to such effect in the famous movie Ryan's Daughter that tourism numbers into the heart of beautiful County Kerry have multiplied ever since.

YARDS
6,975

PAR
72

LOCATION
7 miles/1 km north
west of Tralee

TYPE
Links

EMAIL
info@traleegolfclub.com

WEB
www.traleegolfclub.com

Tralee Bay, County Kerry

The romantic nature of the place is also captured by the names assigned to some of the holes. The Old Castle ruin – after which the dramatic 3rd hole is named – stands at a point on the course where, according to ancient law, balls lost to the ocean are forfeited to one Geoffrey de Clabuill. Folklore has it that he was granted the 'wrecks of the sea' by order of King John.

The par four 5th is called Brendan, named after Saint Brendan the navigator, whose famous voyage is partly depicted in the club's crest. The 7th, Randy, is named in respect of a former meeting place for Smugglers. Then there is Palmer's Peak, where Arnie used to stop awhile during his reconnaissance to enjoy the panorama of the Dingle Peninsula.

Or what of the par three 16th – named Shipwreck – set against the Atlantic Ocean, and where the green stands atop the rusted remnants of many a shipwreck?

Beware you also don't become similarly consigned!

◄ **Banna Strand**
Tralee's breathtaking
location beside the
famous Banna Strand
with the Atlantic surf as
a spectacular backdrop.

The 14th ▷
Tralee's timeless 14th hole, sculpted from some marvellous dunes. The challenge is to play from an elevated tee downwards to a fairway upon which it is essential to avoid deep bunkers tucked into the mounds.

The 16th ▷▷
The 16th, a glorious par three, named 'Shipwreck' which tumbles down to the cliff's edge to a relatively small green overlooking part of the coastline, said locally to be the graveyard of many a doomed ship.

▲ Perfect links land
It is little wonder that course designer Arnold Palmer declared Tralee to be one of the finest natural environments of links land to be found anywhere in the world.

◀ **The 18th**
A spectacular finish away from the sea and played up hill to the backdrop of the clubhouse.
The emphasis is plainly on accuracy as 'The Goat's Hole' contains 13 bunkers. Stay on a left hand route so as to provide the better angle into the green and the chance of a grand finish.
466 yards
Par 4

E

WATERVILLE
GOLF CLUB

Waterville, County Kerry

Proof positive that the links at Waterville is regarded, not just as one of the finest in Ireland, but far beyond, can be readily gleaned by the warming endorsement it continues to acquire from the great players of the day.

Such luminaries as Tiger Woods, Ernie Els, Mark O'Meara and the late Payne Stewart are amongst its many declared admirers. Raymond Floyd was so delighted by his experience that he compared it favourably to Augusta National, Cypress Point, Pebble Beach and the Old Course at St. Andrews.

The prospect now is that Waterville's reputation will grow even further on the strength of renovations carried out by the noted America architect, Tom Fazio.

To make alterations to an already fabled links may be classified as sacrilegious. At the very least it would be carried out with anxious anticipation. Fazio's wise counsel, however, has actually served to restore the former masterpiece. His introduction

YARDS
7,309

PAR
72

LOCATION
1 mile/1.6 kl north
of Waterville village

TYPE
Links

EMAIL
wvgolf@iol.ie

WEB
www.watervillegolfclub.ie

Waterville Bay, Ring of Kerry

of a new par three and four to replace the old and mundane 6th and 7th holes has been widely acclaimed. He has further embellished half a dozen others, each with telling but sensitive craftiness.

It would surely have had the approval of the late John A. Mulcahy. He was the far-sighted Irish-American who became so captivated by what he encountered on a trip around the Ring of Kerry in the mid-1970s, that he commissioned the redoubtable Eddie Hackett to replace a largely defunct nine-hole layout with what today has evolved as one of the world's finest.

Given that the principal elements in the beauty of County Kerry are to be found in its mountains and water, whether in the form of the unpredictable Atlantic or in its shimmering lakes and abundant streams, the dividend for the visitor to Waterville is that these features are readily to hand.

The 17th ▶
A hole that captures the very essence of Waterville – stiff challenge embodied in scenic beauty. John A. Mulcahy insisted that a high-pitched tee be erected on a precise spot so that all who play Waterville can savour and remember its panoramic setting. It's a wholesome 196 yards off the monster blue tee, so creep a little forward if you must so as to be trouble free. Your ball's flight path must traverse a deep gorge, in order to have any prospect of setting up the chance of a par.
196 yards Par 3

With the mountains spread out on one side and Ballinskelligs Bay by the other, your reward is a golfing experience in a picturesque oasis where each captivating hole seems better than the preceding one.

Take the par threes, for instance. Tom Watson has said that Waterville possesses the best par three sequence that he has encountered anywhere on the same golf course. Who would argue, taking account of Fazio's delightful new 6th, the fiendish 12th and the powerful 17th. The latter is an everlasting legacy from the man who discovered a golfer's heaven and kindly invited us to share.

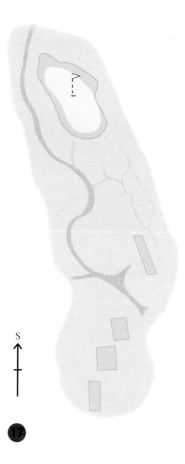

S

◄◄ Mountains and sea

With the multi-hued mountains spread out on one side and the golden sands of Ballinskelligs Bay on the other, Waterville is a picturesque retreat where each captivating hole seems to unfold across the links even better than the preceding one.

◄ The 12th

The view across the 11th fairway to the 12th green – a beautiful par three of 200 yards, known as the Mass Hole, a throwback to penal times in Ireland when local Catholics, fearful of persecution, celebrated Mass in the concealed hollow between the tee and the green.

▼ The 11th

The greatly acclaimed 11th, labelled 'a beautiful monster', which is set in a corridor between classic dunes and with a reputation for its capacity to wreck a card!

IRISH GOLF COURSES

Connacht – West of Ireland

COUNTY GALWAY

Ardacong
ardacong@eircom.net
Sited in leafy grounds of Ardacong House, new back nine is the tougher.

Athenry
athenrygc@eircom.net
www.athenrygolfclub
Parkland/heathland mix with feature par 3's.

Ballinasloe
ballinasloegolfclub@eircom.net
www.ballinasloegolfclub.com
Rolling parkland with many challenging dog-legs.

Bearna
info@bearnagolfclub.com
www.bearnagolfclub.com
Designed by Bobby Browne amidst beauty of Galway Bay and the Burren – toughened by water hazards.

Connemara Isles
padraicoc@eircom.net
Ruddy-Craddock designed unique island nine- hole haven in heart of Connemara Gaeltacht.

Curra West
hcapsec@currawest.com
www.currawest.com
Peaceful setting where greens are well protected.

Dunmore Demesne
ddgc@eircon.net
Shortness counteracted by difficulty of nine holes.

Galway
www.galwaygolf.com
Excellent 18 holes partly by sea-shore with magnificent new clubhouse and panoramic views of Galway Bay.

Galway Bay
www.gbaygolf.com
Enjoys magnificent setting on shores of fabled bay seascape: – true championship test, with on-site hotel.

Glenlo Abbey
info@glenloabbey.ie
www.glenlo.com
Imaginatively created nine holes in hotel grounds.

Gort
info@gortgolf.com
www.golfgolf.com
Re-designed in 1996, being rewarded by increasing reputation.

Loughrea
loughreagolfclub@eircom.net
Short by standards but demanding in challenge, notably on second nine.

Mountbellew
mountbellewgc@eircom.net
Comes strongly recommended - nine holes, 18 tees and a delight to play.

Oughterard
oughterardgc@eircom.net
oughterardgolf.com
New clubhouse complements increasing reputation of re-design in invigorating setting.

Portumna
portumnagc@eircom.net
Laid out in beautiful rolling woodland close to Lough Derg and with telling par 3 as the climax.

Tuam
tuamgolfclub@eircom.net
www.tuamgolfclub.com
New clubhouse to mark 2004 centenary embellishes fine tree-lined lay out where Christy O'Connor Snr was once the resident professional.

COUNTY LEITRIM

Ballinamore
ballinamoregolfclub@eircom.net
www.ballinamoregolfclub.com
One of finest nine holers in the west of Ireland.

COUNTY MAYO

Achill
achillgolfclub@eircom.net
Inviting nine-hole amenity in holiday resort.

Ashford Castle
www.ashford.ie
ashford@ashford.ie
Very pleasant nine holes added amenity in grounds of five-star hotel.

Ballina
ballinagolfhc@eircom.net
www.ballinagolfclub.com
Undulating terrain with water hazards and bonus of stunning vista provided by Ox Mountains and Nephin Range.

Ballinrobe
info@ballinrobegolfclub.com
www.ballinrobegolfclub.com
Set in matured estate with medieval castle, plentiful water and five par 5s!

Ballyhaunis
ballyhaunisgc1@eircom.net
Cunningly bunkered top quality nine-holer including water hazard.

Belmullet (Carne)
www.belmulletgolfclub.ie
www.carnegolflinks.com
Tranquil, classic links by Blacksod Bay worth experiencing.

Castlebar
www.castlebargolfclub.ie
Fabulous 18th hole underlines quality of re-design.

Claremorris
www.claremorrisgolfclub.com
Lake and streams an added hazard, 17th being a telling example.

Mulranny
Stunning backdrop of Clew Bay a powerful addition to pleasant nine holes.

Swinford
regantommy@eircom.net
www.swinfordgolf.com
Bearing the fruits of significant upgrade to greens and bunkering.

Westport
wpgolf@eircom.net
www.golfwestport.com
Acclaimed championship setting in shadow of pilgrim holy mountain Croagh Patrick, containing many highlight holes.

COUNTY ROSCOMMON

Athlone
agcmensclub@eircom.net
Out of bounds a constant threat on undulating, wooded setting in beautiful Hodson Bay.

Ballaghaderreen
ballaghaderreen@golfnet.ie
www.ballaghaderreen.com
Maturing timber and clever bunkering put emphasis on good course management.

Boyle
Invigorating setting amid mountains – nine holes.

Carrick-on-Shannon
www.carrickgolfclub.ie
Eye catching nine holes with ambitions for extension to 18 holes.

Castlerea
Castlereagolf@oceanfree.net
Nine-hole parkland featuring water, not least at feature par 3 4th hole.

Roscommon
rosgolfclub@eircom.net
Spectacular parkland with beautiful variety of mature trees and tee to green water dominated 13th hole.

Strokestown
Welcoming nine-hole venue fondly referred to as 'a smashing little course'.

COUNTY SLIGO

Ballymote
www.ballymotegolfclub.com
Providing excellent test in attractive surroundings.

Enniscrone
enniscronegolf@eircom.net
www.enniscronegolf.com
Situated by Atlantic Ocean at Killala Bay, true traditional links of widespread reputation designed by Eddie Hackett.

Strandhill
strandhillgc@eircom.net
www.strandhillgc.com
Overshadowed in stature by neighbouring Co. Sligo golf club but most enjoyable in its own special way amid delightful views.

Tubbercurry
contact@tubbercurrygolfclub.com
www.tubbercurrygolfclub.com
Fine nine holes amid trees with noble par 3, par 5 finish.

Leinster - East of Ireland

COUNTY CARLOW

Borris
borrisgolfclub@eircom.net
Friendly combat in lovely setting.

Carlow
carlowgolfclub@eircom.net
www.carlowgolfclub.com
Respected as one of finest inland courses in Ireland, its variety and spice traces its origins to famed architect Tom Simpson.

Killerig
contact@jukkerug-golf.ie
www.killerig-golf.ie
Log cabin styled clubhouse and reputation for fine greens – a compelling combination.

Mount Wolseley
www.mountwolseleymembersclub.ie
www.mountwolseleymembersclub.ie
Another fine new Christy O' Connor Jnr creation with added merit of on-site all-embracing hotel complex.

COUNTY DUBLIN

Balbriggan
balgolf@indigo.ie
www.balbriggangolfclub.com
Challenging parkland commanding great views, prospering by constant upgrading.

Balcarrick
balcarr@iol.ie
www.balcarrickgolfclub.com
Visitor friendly club with tough back nine and water in sight at 10 holes!

Beaverstown
info@beaverstown.com
www.beaverstown.com
One time fruit farm, now wonderful golf course in a blossoming orchard setting by shores of estuary.

Beech Park
info@beechpark.ie
www.beechpark.ie
Newly refurbished clubhouse puts added gloss on nice-to-play popular venue.

Christy O'Connor
christyo@indigo.ie
www.christyoconnor.com
Any club named in honour of 'Himself' commands respect, as is the case in this well run and well priced public amenity close to Dublin Airport.

Citywest
tshine@citywesthotel.com
www.citywesthotel.com
Ireland's premier hotel and conference centre is adorned by two marvellous Christy O'Connor Jnr designed state of art courses

Corballis Links
Corballislinks@golfnet.ie
www.golfdublin.com
A must play example of a public pay-for-play concept where expertly maintained links ground provides the best of golf.

Corrstown
info@corrstowngolfclub.com
www.corrstowngolfclub.com
Two choices: championship standard River Course boasting 18 excellent holes or nine-hole Orchard Course.

Deer Park
dpgcmail@eircom.net
www.deerparkgolfclub.ie
The boast of being Ireland's largest golf complex fits well when you consider that you have the choice of an 18-hole course, two separate nine-hole courses, and an 18-hole pitch and putt facility - all in the grounds of a top class hotel and leisure centre.

Donabate
info@donabategolfclub.com
www.donabategolfclub.com
Top grade 27-hole facility with sand based greens and spanking new clubhouse.

Dublin City
info@dublincitygolf.com
www.dublincitygolf.com
Set in valley of Glen Na Smól (The Valley of the Thrush), where creative redesign work has been sketched by well-known Irish artist Frank Clarke.

Dublin Mountain
dmgc@eircom.net
Rewarding undulating course, coming on strongly in maturity and reputation where visitors are especially welcome.

Dun Laoghaire
dlgc@iol.ie
www.dunlaoghairegolfclub.ie
Planning for a re-location to a 27-hole omplex in lovely Ballyman Glen, south County Dublin.

Forrest Little
francis@forrestlittle.ie
www.forrestlittle.ie
Designed by Fred Hawtree within sight of runways at Dublin Airport – a good test of golf in typical parkland setting.

Foxrock
fgc@indigo.ie
www.foxrockgolfclub.com
Short nine holes in sylvan south county Dublin with forbidding opening tee shot!

Glencullen
admin@glencullengolfclub.ie
www.glencullengolfclub.ie
Nine-hole treat on Dublin mountainside commanding wonderful views below.

Hermitage
info@thehermitage.com
Golfing haven on western outskirts of Dublin city, handsomely upgraded and with many key holes – not least the short 10th downhill to banks of River Liffey.

Hibernian
hiberniangolf@eircom.net
www.hiberniangolf.com
Well run members club is in association with City West courses facilities.

Hollywood Lakes
Hollywoodlakesgc@eircom.net;
www.hollywoodlakesgolfclub.com
Appropriately named Mel Flanagan design, given that water impacts at half of the holes.

Killiney
killineygolfclub@eircom.net
Perched on side of Killiney Hill, delightful nine holes parkland boasts unrivalled views of south County Dublin – and beyond.

Lucan
lucangolf@eircom.net
www.lucangolfclub.ie
Nice short undulating course finishing with two par 5's.

Malahide
malgc@club.ie
www.malahidegolfclub.ie
Enticing well settled 27-hole complex, with superb clubhouse facilities.

Roganstown
golf@roganstown.com
www.roganstown.com
Peaceful lakes, rolling hills and with a luxury hotel on site, the Broadmeadow River flows beside the course and water comes into play on all but six holes.

Rush
info@rushgolfclub.com
Strongly recommended where old world charm endures at quaint-nine hole links.

St. Margaret's
reservations@stmargaretsgolf.com
www.stmargaretsgolf.com
A Ruddy-Craddock design of distinction offering tough test and challenge of many water features, most notably at 12th and 18th holes.

Skerries
skerriesgolfclub@eircom.net
www.skerriesgolfclub.ie
New hole introduction has brought reward of new stature, highlighted by dramatic downhill dog leg 18th beside refurbished clubhouse.

Slade Valley
sladevalleygc@eircom.net
Rich compensation of panoramic views for steep climbs around forgiving lay out.

South County
info@southcogolf.ie
www.southcountygolf.ie
Designer Nick Bielenberg has astutely weaved a good pattern on undulating terrain where water features are cleverly utilised.

Swords Open
swordsgc@indigo.ie
www.swordsopengolfcourse.com
By the banks of the Broadmeadow River, recommended for good green fee value.

Turvey
info@turveygolfclub.com
www.turveygolfclub.com
Inspired design in wooded setting by ex-European tour pro, Paddy McGuirk.

Westmanstown
info@westmanstowngolfclub.ie
www.westmanstowngolfclub.ie
Improving with age and upgrade work.

DUBLIN CITY

Ballinascorney
info@ballinascorneygolfclub.com
www.ballinascorneygolfclub.com
Sloping nine holes in Glenasmole valley, more difficult than yardages might suggest.

Carrickmines
carrickminesgolf@eircom.net
Set on a choice site on hilly terrain, provides a pleasurable mix in nine hole challenge.

Castle
info@castlegc.ie;www.cstlegc.ie
Well manicured one time orchard with boasts to have early design inspiration by professionals Barcroft, Pickman and Hood.

Castleknock Golf Club
E-mail: monarchproperties@eircom.net
Web: www.castleknockgolfclub.ie
New 18-hole Jonathan Gaunt design, built to top specification standards.

Clontarf
Info.cgc@indigo.ie
www.clontarfgolfclub.ie
Oasis within drive and pitch of Dublin city, popular course makes up for lack of length by onus on accuracy.

Edmondstown
info@edmondstowngolfclub.ie
www.edmondstowngolfclub.ie
Completely upgraded in 2002 with interesting new lay out which is kept in very good condition.

Elm Park
office@elmparkgolfclub.ie
www.elmparkgolfclub.ie
Showing all the benefits of a face-lift under the expert guidance of architect Patrick Merrigan, while maintaining special charm in beautiful ambience.

Elmgreen
elmgreen@golfdublin.com
www.golfdublin.com
Popular well run municipal facility with fine 18-hole course, floodlit driving range and pitch and putt lay out.

Grange
administration@grangegolfclub.ie
www.grangegolfclub.ie
Stands out for its beautifully wooded setting, its six par 3s, par of 68 – and punishing test!

Grange Castle
info@grangeca-castle.com
www.grange-castle.com
Another commendable example of local council providing excellent Public course facilities – always in the best of condition.

Hazel Grove
hazelgroveladies@hotmail.com
5,361 yards, 67 par on hilly terrain with special welcome for visitors.

Hollystown
info@hollytstown.com
www.hollystown.com
Exuding all that's best within surroundings of trees, lakes and streams, three nine-hole loops presents multiple playing choices.

Howth
manager@howthgolfclub.ie
www.howthgolfclub.ie
Captivating views overlooking Dublin Bay on distinctive parkland/heathland hillside demanding accurate placement at all times.

Kilmashogue
kilmashoguegc@eircom.net
Short and pleasurable nine holes nestling in wooded grounds of St Columba's College.

Luttrellstown
luttrellstownmensgc@eircom.net
www.luttrellstowngc.com
Major re-development work will further enhance reputation of lovely golfing environment with Castle hotel facilities and unique clubhouse.

Milltown
info@miltowngolfclub.ie
www.miltowngolfclub.ie
Lovely, Century – old suburban refuge amid strong foliage with good hole variation.

Newlands
atonngc@eircom.net
Another James Braid original offering a great challenge in invigorating setting.

Rathfarnham
rgc@oceanfree.net
14-hole picturesque setting in foothills of Dublin Mountains, with original nine-hole design by esteemed John Jacobs.

St. Anne's
info@stanneslinksgolf.com
www.stanneslinksgolf.ie
True links neighbour of Royal Dublin GC deserving its own distinction following major course and clubhouse improvements.

Stackstown
stackstowngc@eircom.net
www.stackstowngolfclub.com
High set by the Dublin Mountains with uninterrupted views of Dublin City and its Bay – and where leading world-ranked professional Padraig Harrington learned to play.

Sutton
menshandicaps@suttongolfclub.org
www.suttongolfclub.org
Tight nine-hole links with fine clubhouse encompassing Joe Carr room in salute of one of Ireland's greatest amateurs and golfing ambassadors.

COUNTY KILDARE

Athy
info@athygolfclub.com
www.athygolfclub.com
With new clubhouse arrival in 2003, now a quality venue with fearsome back nine climax.

Bodenstown
bodenstown@eircom.net
36–hole complex set amongst mature trees in tranquil surroundings.

Castlewarden
info@castlewardengolfclub.com
www.castlewardengolfclub.com
Designed by Tommy Halpin and the late Tom Craddock, end result is a searching test with some lakes to encounter.

Celbridge Elm Hall
Inviting nine holes and good value for money.

Cill Dara
cilldaragc@eircom.net
An enchanting well worth visiting nine holes alongside famous Curragh race course, many of whose members are of the horse-racing fraternity.

Clane
clanegolfclub@iolfree.ie
www.clanegolfclub.ie
Sited on the grounds of Clongowes Wood College, short but fulfilling nine holes.

Clongowes Wood College
Short and satisfying nine-hole extra curricular school amenity.

Craddockstown
registar@craddockstown.com
A maturing Arthur Spring design with lakes a prominent feature.

Curragh
curraghgolf@tinet.ie
Golf dates back to 1883 where the game might first have been played: tough long course with many feature holes in bracing setting.

Highfield
highfieldgolfclub@eircom.net
Quality family run complex, embracing excellent course in pleasant setting, plus floodlit practice facilities.

Kilkea Castle
kilkeacastlegc@eircom.net
Impressive Castle Hotel/Golf Club combination making astute usage of River Greese and where the 12th century castle is on view from all fairways.

Killeen
admin@killeengc.ie
Par 72, 6800-yard course of full USGA specification – deserves growing reputation.

Knockanally
golf@knockanally.com
www.knockanally.com
Stately setting with 19th century Palladian mansion for clubhouse and strong selection of holes, not least the foreboding first!

Millicent
info@millicentgolfclub.com
www.millicentgolfclub.com
Has made rapid progress in maturity and reputation since 2001 opening of wonderfully groomed and run parkland set in ideal landscape with water a strategically placed danger, especially on make-or-break 17th.

Naas
nasgolfclubisdn@eircom.net
www.naasgolfclub.ie
Tree-lined fairways to well protected greens surrounded by bunkers and some water underlines the challenge.

Newbridge
newbridgegolfclub@eircom.net
www.newbridgegolfclub.com
Year on year improvements programme working a treat with 40,000 tree plantation maturing and water features an added obstacle.

Woodlands
woodlandsgolf@eircom.net
www.woodlandsgolf.ie
Now extended to 18 holes, offering a fulfilling experience.

COUNTY KILKENNY

Callan
info@callangolfclub.com
www.callangolfclub.com
Extended to full 18 in 1999 and remembered for friendliness and lurking stream!

Castlecomer
castlecomergolf@eircom.net
www.castlecomergolf.com
Set in 200-year-old forest and improved enormously by Ruddy re-design.

Gowran Park
gowranpk@eircom.net
Set within famous race course, a Jeff Howes design of true quality.

Kilkenny
enquiries@kilkennygolfclub.com
www.kinkennygolfclub.com
Extensively modified to enhance reputation as one of Ireland's most pleasant inland courses.

Mountain View
info@mviewgolf.com
www.mviewgolf.com
Large lake in play at four holes of course designed on plateau giving breathtaking views.

Waterford
info@waterfordgolfclub.com
www.waterfordgolfclub.com
Attractive high perched parkland course designed by legendary British Open champion James Braid.

COUNTY LAOIS

Abbeyleix
info@abbeyleixgolfclub.ie
www.abbeyleixgolf.ie
A venue of much renown favourably refurbished by design expert Mel Flanagan.

The Heath
info@theheathgc.ie
www.theheathgc.ie
Strangely unsung considering merit on good dry ground and stiff test incorporating lake.

Mountrath

mountrathgc@eircom.net
www.mountrathgolfclub.ie
Extended tees, new greens and water features provide upgrade against trademark backdrop of Bloom Mountains.

Portarlington

portarlingtongc@eircom.net
www.portarlingtongolf.com
Showing all the fruits of extension to 18 holes in renowned sylvan setting and featuring a game bird sanctuary.

Rathdowney

rathdowneygolf@eircom.net
www.rathdowneygolfclub.com
Perseverance by the members for constant review and upgrade down the years has produced a proud course to compare with most of its type.

COUNTY LONGFORD

County Longford

colonggolf@eircom.net
Newly re-vamped by architect Mel Flanagan, undulating parkland strengthened by some water features.

COUNTY LOUTH

Ardee

ardeegolfclub@eircom.net
www.ardeegolfclub.com
Good test of golf with tight fairways between plentiful trees and well-bunkered greens.

Carnbeg

Quality pay-as-you-play concept against panoramic backdrop of Cooley Mountains.

Dundalk

nabager@dundalkgolfclub.ie
www.dundalkgolfclub.ie
Enjoys superb scenic vistas and enhanced reputation following upgrade by the formidable team of Peter Alliss and Dave Thomas.

Greenore

greenoregolfclub@eircom.net
Beside Carlingford Lough on Cooley Peninsula, old established links enhanced by welcoming new clubhouse.

Killinbeg

killinbeggolfclub@eircom.net
Nice to play, low cost giving good value for money.

Seapoint

golflinks@seapoint.ie
www.seapointgolfclub.com
Highly rated, largely links with some water hazards.

Townley Hall

townleyhall@oceanfree.net
Nine holes with historical connotations given it is on site of the Battle of the Boyne.

COUNTY MEATH

Ashbourne

ashgc@iol.ie
www.ashbournegolfclub.ie

Water in play at 50 per cent of holes and further danger lurks around 'Amen Corner' – between the 11th and 14th.

Black Bush

golf@blackbush.iol.ie
www.blackbushgolf.ie
27-hole high quality facility offering varying challenges in mature bracing setting.

County Meath

sec@trimgolf.net
www.trimgolf.net
Always maintained to high standard and offering great variety of holes and shots.

Gormanston College

info@gormanstowncollege.ie
www.gormanstoncollege.ie
Commendable nine-hole facility in school grounds

Headfort

hgeadmin@eircom.net
www.headfortgolfclub.ie
One of finest parkland settings in Ireland offering a choice of two courses, the more recent dramatic stand-out creation being widely acclaimed.

Kilcock

www.kilcockgolfclub.com
Undulating, well-kept greens, many trees and much water combine in an agreeable challenge.

Laytown and Bettystown

links@kabdv.ie;www.landb.ie
Commanding stretch of good linksland on which Ryder Cup ace Des Smyth learned his trade.

Moore Park

billcarney@eircom.net
Green fee based facility offering honest value for money.

Navan

info@navangolfclub.ie
www.navangolfclub.ie
Popular visitor-orientated course situated within Navan Racecourse.

Rathcore

info@rathcoregolfcandcountryclub.com
www.rathcoregolfandcountryclub.com
Water at 12 holes underpins dangers on wonderful new concept by designer Mel Flanagan and contoured imaginatively by Lyons brothers, Mick and Austin.

Royal Tara

info@royaltaragolfclub.com
www.royaltaragolfclub.com
Lush course close to historic Hill of Tara offering honest challenge to all standards.

South Meath

smgc@eircom.net
www.southmeathgolfclub.com
Inexpensive to play and encourages a bold approach – but beware!

Summerhill

namadrarua@eircom.net
Nine-hole parkland in lovely setting – visitors welcome.

COUNTY OFFALY

Beechlawn

beechlwngolf@eircom.net
None too expensive to play and with driving range.

Birr

birrgolfclub@eircom.net
Superb - but not given due recognition - golf course with facilities to match.

Castle Barna

info@castlebarna.ie
www.castlebarna.ie
Enjoyable offering by Grand Canal amidst mature trees, streams and easygoing terrain.

Edenderry

enquiries@edenderrygolfclub.com
www.edenderrygolfclub.com
Laid on springy turf surface, offers stout examination of shot making.

Esker Hills

info@eskerhillsgolf.com
www.eskerhillsgolf.com
Lots of thrills in store throughout hilly terrain spiced with woodlands and lakes.

Tullamore

tullamoregolfclub@eircom.net
www.tullamoregolf.ie
Handsomely modernised course of real merit set amidst some of the oldest and finest tree species.

COUNTY WESTMEATH

Ballinlough Castle

golf@ballinloughcastle.com
www.ballinloughcastle.com
Low priced green fee, now upgraded to full 18 holes of high spec standards.

Delvin Castle

delvincastle@golfnet.ie
Interesting mix of holes played against startling backdrop of historic Cloyne Castle.

Glasson

info@glassongolf.ie
www.glassongolf.ie
Magical setting overlooking River Shannon's Lough Ree, with exceptional par 5, 14th tumbling to lake shore, followed by apprehension of par 3, 15th to an island green.

Moate

moategolfclub@eircom.net
www.moategolfclub.ie
Ever friendly and welcoming, set in gently rolling parkland with some narrow target areas.

Mount Temple

Mttemple@iol.ie
www.mounttemplegolfclub.ie
'Built by God, polished by Man' is club's proud boast of this quite handsome course – find out!

Mullingar

mullingargolfclub@hotmail.com
www.mullingargolfclub.ie
Has prospered following cosmetic work down

the years, but essentially the product of famous architect James Braid, the telling par 3 second from elevated tee to an elevated green being one of his enduring trademarks.

COUNTY WEXFORD

Courtown

info@courtowngolfclub.com
www.courtowngolfclub.com
Premium not on length – but on accuracy in favourite seaside resort.

Enniscorthy

engc@eircom.net
More challenging now following successful re-design.

New Ross

newrossgolf@eircom.net
www.newrossgolfclub.net
Clever playing strategy demanded throughout.

Rosslare

office@rosslaregolf.com
www.rosslaregolf.com
True championship links in stature and thriving in a popular holiday destination.

Seafield

info@seafieldgolf.com
www.seafieldgolf.com
Blend of parkland, heathland and links combines in a fascinating new cliff top concept complemented by top quality clubhouse facilities.

St. Helen's Bay

sthelensgolfclub@eircom.net.
Nine water features and 5,000 trees tells their own story on this Philip Walton design, where 14 holes overlook the coastline. On site cottage accommodation adds to amenity in holiday resort.

Tara Glen

gerardm@microsoft.com
Fun to play nine-hole holiday course in stunning location beside beach.

Wexford

info@wexfordgolfclub.ie
www.wexfordgolfclub.ie
Distinctive and well liked with additional benefit of views to Saltee Islands and Blackstairs Mountains.

COUNTY WICKLOW

Arklow

arklowgolflinks@eircom.net
www.arklowgolflinks.com
Largely unsung links where original nine holes design by five times British Open champion John Taylor have been adorned with nine new ones by the hand of Eddie Hackett.

Baltinglass

info@baltinglassgc.com
www.baltinglassgc.com
Addition of new nine by designer Eddie Connaughton has upped reputation of popular club on banks of River Slaney.

Blainroe
blainroegolfclub@eircom.net
www.blainroe.com
Stimulating sea views enriches experience of competing on Hawtree design.

Boystown
boystowngc@eircom.net
Agreeable nine-hole challenge where some water keeps you alert.

Bray
braygolfclub@eircom.net
www.braygolfclub.com
New scenically located course designed by Smyth and Brannigan gives club new stature at popular sea side tourist town where, it is claimed, the first verifiable playing of golf in Ireland took place in about 1762.

Charlesland
golf@charlesland.com
www.charlesland.com
CV adorned by designer Eddie Hackett where many holes scenically overlook the Irish Sea.

Coollatin
coollatingolfclub@eircom.net
www.coollatingolfclub.com
Enjoying new status since Peter McEvoy designed additional nine.

Delgany
delganygolf@eircom.net
www.delganygolfclub.com
Helped by some design suggestions from the esteemed Harry Vardon, course has sustained a high reputation for shot examination and scenic peaceful surrounds.

Djouce
djoucegcm@eircom.net
Ironically level nine-hole course between Dublin and Wicklow mountains.

Glen of the Downs
info@glenofthedown.com
www.glenofthedowns.com
Scenic parkland with links features built to top specifications and highlighted by collection of notable par 3s – and superb clubhouse.

Glenmalure
www.glenmaluregolf.com
Another County Wicklow course exacting full visual dividends of placement within the Vale of Avoca.

Greystones
secretary@greystonesgc.com
www.greystonesgc.com
Compatible mix of old and new holes in fabulously wooded and scenic setting.

Kilcoole
Kilcoolemens@eircom.net
www.kilcoolegolfclub.com
Nine holes that nobly play part in proud Co. Wicklow golf reputation – watch out for feature island hole.

Kilternan
kgc@kilternan-hotel.ie
www.kilternangolfandcountryclub.com
Hillside course with added hotel and ski slop practice facilities!

Old Conna
info@oldconna.com
www.oldconna.ie
Combines panoramic sea and mountain views in exceptional setting beautifully embroidered by architect Eddie Hackett.

Roundwood
rwood@indigo.ie
www.roundwoodgolf.com
Forceful course in stunning mountain/sea setting with superb clubhouse.

Tulfarris
tomopine@eircom.net
www.tulfarris.com
Magnificent hotel and golf resort where architect Patrick Merrigan has meticulously extracted the best from dramatic setting overlooking Blessington Lakes.

Vartry Lakes
vartrylakes@hotmail.com
www.wicklow.ie
Visitor friendly, tough nine holes adjoining lakes in beautiful Roundwood.

Wicklow
newsite@wicklowgolfclub.com
info@wicklowgolfclub.com
On cliff top overlooking Wicklow Bay with par 3 features and scenic landscape the locals claim to be best in Ireland!

Woodbrook
golf@woodbrook.ie
www.woodbrook.ie
Has regained its old glory and high place in pecking order on strength of major course and clubhouse refurbishment.

Woodenbridge
wgc@eircom.net
www.woodenbridge.com
River and lake intrude to magnify examination in lovely sylvan surroundings.

Munster - South of Ireland

COUNTY CLARE

Clonlara
markmorris@iol.ie
Amenable nine holes where accuracy rather than length is premium.

Portstewart

East Clare
eastclaregolfclub@eircom.net
www.eastclare.com
Lakes, bunkers, streams and trees await on this quality pay–as–you–play facility.

Ennis
egc@eircom.net
www.ennisgolfclub.com
Fabulous new clubhouse enhances immaculately manicured tree-lined course in busy holiday area.

Kilkee
kilkeegolfclub@eircom.net
www.kilkeegolfclub.ie
Rugged links course with splendid cliff top views over the Atlantic.

Kilrush
info@kilrushgolfclub.com
www.kilrushgolfclub.com
Beautifully positioned, looking out on the River Shannon, the Kerry Mountains and Atlantic Ocean.

Shannon
shannongolfclub@eircom.net
www.shannongolf.com
Flat but long and challenging alongside runways of Shannon international airport.

Spanish Point
dkfitzgerald@tinet.ie
www.spanishpointgolf.com
Classic old hilly nine-hole links with some tantalising par 3s.

Woodstock
gsadlier@data-display.com
www.woodstockgolfclub.com
Gaining big reputation for interesting challenge amidst trees, rivers and lake.

COUNTY CORK

Bandon
bandongolfclub@eircom.net
Long established upright test in pleasant ambience, noted for prevalence of bird species.

Bantry Bay
info@bantrygolf.com
www.bantrygolf.com
Epitomises the beauty of West Cork in stunning setting where majority of holes overlook the shores of the Bay.

Berehaven
admin@berehavengolf.com
www.berehavengolf.com
Overlooking Bantry Bay, a nine-hole combination of parkland and links with sea water a constant feature.

Blarney
blarneygolf@esatbiz.com
www.blarneygolfcourse.com
Backboned by spectacular water-orientated par 3s at sixth and 16th.

Charleville
charlevillegolf@eircom.net
www.charlevillegolf.com
27-hole complex in woods on foothills of Ballyhoura Mountain range and a most welcoming club.

Cobh
m.lynch@irc.ie
Public parkland nine-hole course in famous holiday seaport.

Coosheen
coosheengolfclub@eircom.net
http:homepage.eircom.net/~coosheengc
Overlooks picturesque Schull Harbour in West Cork, opens with three par 3s!

Cork
corkgolfclub@eircom.net
www.corkgolfclub.ie
Designed by legendary Alister Mackenzie and popularly known as Little Island – classic high merit mature parkland.

Doneraile
Little nine-hole parkland where river comes into play.

Douglas
admin@douglasgolfclub.com
www.douglasgolfclub.ie
Perched scenically on elevated site on outskirts of Cork City – high class amenity toughened by alterations.

Dunmore
dunmoremens@eircom.net
Adjacent to Dunmore House Hotel, friendly nine holes overlooking Atlantic.

East Cork
eastcorkgolfclub@eircom.net
www.eastcorkgolfclub.com
Heavily tree-lined and where Ownacurragh River supplies water hazards.

Fermoy
fermoygolfclub@eircom.net
Founded in 1892 and situated off main Dublin-Cork road, undulating heathland amidst profusion of heather and gorse.

Fernhill
fernhill@golfnet.ie
Fine facility over looking handsome Owenabwee Valley, with adjoining hotel complex.

Fota Island
www.fotaisland.com
Good enough to host Irish Open championships in 2001 and 2002 and adjacent to noted Wild Life Park – a wonderful addition to Ireland's many new concepts.

Frankfield
frankfield@golfnet.ie
Family run 9-hole hilly parkland course with stunning views over Cork City.

Glengarriff
glengarriffgolfgents@eircom.net
Short but challenging nine-hole parkland vies for distinction of having most scenic setting in Ireland.

Harbour Point
hpoint@iol.ie
www.harbourpointgolfclub.com
High above Cork's sweeping landscape, matured into course that offers serious challenge.

Kanturk
kanturkgolfclub@eircom.net
www.kanturkgolf.com
Demands accuracy amidst mature plantation.

Kinsale
kinsalegolf.com
www.kinsalegolf.com
Comes in two choices: the old 9-hole course at Ringanane which overlooks the sea and has panoramic views, and the new rolling hills, more difficult 18-hole course at Farrangalway.

Lee Valley
leevalley@golfnet.ie
www.leevalleygcc.ie.
Renowned for its spectacular scenery.

Lisselan
info@lisselan.com
www.lisselan.com
Unique by the way the course comprises just six holes, played three times from differing tee boxes. Exceptional too in unusual attraction of raft ride across river Argideen from fourth fairway to green!

Macroom
mcroomgc@iol.ie
Restful parkland setting in castle grounds, with half a dozen holes alongside water.

Mahon
mahon@golfnet.ie
Marvellous example of how top class municipal facilities can be made available for non club members.

Mallow
golfmall@gofree.indigo.ie
Majestic rural setting which has prospered from constant upgrading.

Mitchelstown
info@mitchelstown-golf.com
www.mitchelstown-golf.com
Galtee Mountains provide charming backdrop for test that can bite!

Monkstown
office@monkstowngolfclub.com
www.monkstowngolfclub.com
Made all the more difficult by new bunkering and water features, especially tough last two holes.

Muskerry
muskgc@eircom.net
Physically demanding with some steep climbs, but richly compensated for in scenic value and thrill of final four holes with river in sight.

Raffeen Creek
www.raffeencreekgolfclub.com
Fine nine holes highlighted by water feature on last two.

Skibbereen
skibbmen@skibbgolf.com
www.skibbgolf.com
Beware the threat of 'Amen Corner' in lovely blend of old and new nines.

Water Rock
waterrock@eircom.net
www.waterrockgolfcourse.com
240 yards, 12th hole over Swan Lake to well bunkered green illustrates nature of test.

Youghal
youghalgolfclub@eircom.net
www.youghalgolf.com
A quality added amenity on hilltop by famous medieval seaside town presenting great variety of shots.

COUNTY KERRY

Ardfert
ardfertgolfclub@eircom.net
Opened since 1994 and popular with visitors – flat but deceptive nine holes.

Ballyheigue Castle
ballyheiguecgc@eircom.net
www.kerryweb/destination-kerry/ballyheigue/golfclub.htmi
Parkland nine holes in mature woodland surrounding eighteenth century castle.

Beaufort
beaufortgolfclub@eircom.net
www.beaufortgolfclub.net
Set against the backdrop of spectacular Macgillycuddy Reeks mountain range and with stone built clubhouse – a rich experience.

Castlegregory
castlegregorygolf@oceanfree.net
Home of the near extinct Natterjack toad in heart of Dingle Peninsula, nine holes links restored by Arthur Spring in most scenic sea-side location.

Castleisland
managercastleislandgolfclub@eircom.net
www.castleislandgolfclub.com
New parkland creation built to highest specifications in wooded setting.

Castlerosse
reservations@crhk.ie
www.castlerossehotelkillarney.com
Nine holes in grounds of hotel of the same name, with similar ambience to adjoining Killarney's illustrious Killeen course.

Ceann Sibeal
dinglegc@iol.ie
www.dinglelinks.com
Located far west (with claims to be most westerly in Europe!) on the Dingle Peninsula, a classic, if unheralded, panoramic links.

Dooks
office@dooks.com
www.dooks.com
Golf has been played here on traditional links since 1889. Popular upgraded venue in holiday area.

Dunloe
enquiries@dunloegc.com
www.dunloegc.com
Stands out for its spectacular views of Killarney's lakes and mountains from all nine holes.

Kenmare
info@kenmaregolfclub.com
www.kenmaregolfclub.com
Challenging but fair, well-sheltered course, very scenic.

Kerries
thekerriesgolfcourse@eircom.net
Nine-hole parkland course offering attraction of wonderful views of Tralee Bay, the Slieve Mish Mountains and Dingle Peninsula.

Killorglin
kilgolf@iol.ie
www.killorglingolf.ie
Overlooking Dingle Bay with stimulating views of Macgillycuddy Reeks from every fairway.

Listowel
listowelgc@eircom.net
Lots of trees running down the centre of this nine-hole course where lovely river Feale is also a feature.

Parknasilla
parknasilla@golfnet.ie
Lovable 12-hole course in grounds of famous hotel overlooking Kenmare Bay.

Ring of Kerry
reservations@ringofderrygolf.com
www.ringofkerrygolf.com
Commands envied scenic landscape high above Kenmare Bay and with some spectacular hole designs to match.

Ross
rossgolfclub@eircom.net
www.rossgolfclub.com
Mountains, woodland, water – a nine-hole offering which typifies beauty of County Kerry.

COUNTY LIMERICK

Abbeyfeale
abbeyfealegolf@eircom.net
Undemanding and hospitable – what better combination!

Castletroy
Cgc@iol.ie
www.castletroygolfclub.ie
In existence since 1937, commands great respect as charming tree-lined venue with excellent facilities.

Limerick
lgc@eircom.net
www.limerickgc.com
Venerable old club in mature parkland, encompassing design concepts by Alister Mackenzie and John D. Harris.

Limerick County
lcmens@eircom.net
www.limerickco.com
Des Smyth designed with added amenities of Academy and on-site cottage accommodation.

Newcastle West
ncwgolf@eircom.net
Richly varied new course designed by Arthur Spring to best quality specifications.

Rathbane
rathbanegolfclub@eircom.net
Noted for its competitive rates and visitor friendly flavour.

COUNTY TIPPERARY

Ballykisteen
www.ballykisteen.com
Designed by United States Champions tour star Des Smyth, 18 holes on rolling parkland with stream adding to difficulty.

Cahir Park
management@cahirparkgolfclub.com
www.cahirparkgolf.com
Crosses River Suir on two holes and where water comes into play at seven holes in all! Fine clubhouse adds to inviting package.

Clonmel
cgc@indigo.ie
www.clonmelgolfclub.com
Beautiful and challenging in spectacular setting.

County Tipperary (Dundrum House)
dundrumgolf@eircom.net
www.dundrumhousehotel.com
Designed by Ryder Cup star Philip Walton, an exhilarating par 72 tough test by Multeen River, laid out in hotel grounds.

Nenagh
nenaghgolfclub@eircom.net
www.nenaghgolfclub.com
Superb design highlighting clever bunkering and water hazards – hospitable 19th. hole is a just reward!

Rockwell College
Private course in school grounds.

Roscrea
www.roscreagolfclub.ie
Agreeable parkland 18 holes with many par 3s and challenge of 'Burma Road'!

Slievenamon
info@slievenamongolfclub.com
www.slievenamongolfclub.com
Grand pay-and-play concept situated in the beautiful valley of Slievenamon.

Templemore
Tmoregc1@eircom.net
Scenic view of Devil's Bit Mountain and another bite in opening and closing par 5s.

Thurles
thurlesgolf@eircom.net
Scoring on the par 3s takes a priority in well liked prime parkland location.

Tipperary
tipperarygolfclub@eircom.net
Where once there were no hazards, bunkers and water are now central in impressive extension and upgrade.

COUNTY WATERFORD

Carrick on Suir
Info@carrickgolfclub.com
www.carrickgolfclub.com
Founded in 1939 and now extended to full 18, commands breathtaking views of Comeragh Mountains and Suir Valley.

Dungarvan
dungarvangc@eircom.net
www.dungarvangolfclub.com
Enjoys lovely setting and presents tough test amid many strategically placed lakes!

Dunmore East
dunmoregolf@eircom.net
www.dunmore-golf.com
Coastal setting overlooking fishing village of Dunmore East, with breathtaking vista.

Faithlegg
fgc@eircom.net
www.faithlegg.com
Created by top architect Paddy Merrigan in lush 200-acre estate with quality hotel on site – excellent new facility.

Goldcoast
Goldcoastgolfclub1@eircom.net
www.goldcoastgolfclub.com
Extended to 18 holes, it presents a good mix in popular tourist area.

Lismore
lismoregolfclub@eircom.net
9-hole parkland set in the beautiful and venerable grounds of Lismore Castle.

Tramore
tragolf@iol.ie
www.tramoregolfclub.com
Offers all standards a fair test in varied mature wooded setting close to popular seaside tourist resort.

Waterford Castle
waterfordcastle@eircom.net
www.waterfordcastle.com
Unique in that its island location is accessible only by ferry, a magnificently varied Des Smyth design and accompanying Castle hotel, presents special package.

West Waterford
info@westwaterfordgolf.com
www.westwaterfordgolf.com
Spread over 150 acres of rolling parkland on the banks of the Brickey River, offering great value.

Williamstown
williamstowngolfclub@eircom.net
By the design hand of the great Eddie Hackett, another example of excellent municipal course facilities

Ulster – North of Ireland

COUNTY ANTRIM

Antrim
antrimgc@btinternet.com
www.antrimgolfclub.com
Three lakes provide troublesome danger on front nine.

Ballycastle
info@ballycastlegolfclub,.com
www.ballycastlegolfclub.com
Venerable 1890 construction with inland/links mix and fabulous views.

Ballyclare
ballyclaregolfclub@supanet.com
www.ballyclaregolfclub.net.
Water stalks amid tree-lined fairways.

Ballymena
ballymena@golfnet.ie
Short by standards but tough going in shadow of Slemish Mountain of St. Patrick fame.

Burnfield House
michaelhj@ntlworld.com
www.burnfieldhousegolfclub.co.uk
Good conditioned, tricky parkland nine holer.

Bushfoot
bushfootgolfclub@btconnect.com
Long established links set in outstanding beauty.

Cairndhu
cairndhu@utvinternet.com
Take time to enjoy views in most picturesque setting.

Carrickfergus
carrickfergusgc@btconnect.com
Showing all the dividends of major refurbishment.

Cushendall
Cushendall.golfclub@virgin.net
Delightful 9 holes nestling on shores of Red Bay in beautiful Glens of Antrim.

Down Royal
info@downroyalgolfclub.com
www.downroyalgolfclub.com
Situated within Down Royal (Maze) race course on dry heathland.

Gracehill
info@gracehillgolfclub.co.uk
www.fgracehillgolfclub.co.uk
Added difficulty in that many greens are by side of water hazards.

Greenacres
johndoagh@aol.com
www.greenacresgolfclub.co.uk
Threat of lakes at half a dozen holes on thriving complex, including floodlit golf range.

Greenisland
Greenisland.golf@virgin.net
Look out for delicate challenge of 92-metre eighth hole!

Hilton Templepatrick
Lynn.mccool@hilton.com
www.hilton.com
Four star hotel complex features class new challenging course in mature parkland.

Lambeg
lambeggolfclub@utvinternet.com
Fun to play council run public amenity with six par 3s and no 5s!

Larne
Internet@larnegolfclub.freeserve.co.uk
www.larnegolfclub.co.uk
Magnificent nine-hole setting on Islandmagee Peninsula with panoramic views to the west coast of Scotland.

Lisburn
info@lisburngolfclub.com
www.lisburngolfclub.com.
Tidy parkland by Lagan Valley with dramatic par 3 to finish.

Mallusk
kevinmcglennon@aol.com
Nine hole Belfast City Council run, offering golf at lowest charges in Northern Ireland.

Massereene
info@massereene.com
www.massereene.com
Two distinctive nines alongside lovely Lough Neagh.

Rathmore
Dwilliamson555@btconnect.com
Unobtrusive, welcoming and proud neighbour of more famous Royal Portrush.

Whitehead
r.patrick@qub.ac.uk
Part seaside, part parkland enjoying deserved growing reputation for golf and scenic locale.

COUNTY ARMAGH

Ashfield
www.freespace.virgin.net/ashfield.golfing
Evolving impressively following addition of trees and lakes.

Cloverhill
info@cloverhillgc.com
www.cloverhillgc.com
Now extended to 18 holes and with river in play.

Co. Armagh
info@golfarmagh.co.uk
www.golfarmagh.co.uk
Beautiful and friendly – what more could you ask?

Loughgall
Astute Don Patterson design in mature woodland with water an added feature.

Lurgan
lurgangolfclub@utvinternet.com
www.lurgangolfclub.co.uk
Regarded as one of best inland courses in Northern Ireland, with stunning views over Lurgan Park Lake.

Portadown
portadowngc@btconnect.com
www.portadowngolfclub.co.uk
On banks of River Bann which comes regularly into play.

Silverwood
kierandevlin@fsmail.net
Hotel complex 18-hole course, nine hole par 3, floodlit range and pitch and putt course.

Tandragee
Office@tandragee.co.uk
www.tandragee.co.uk
Formidable and picturesque amid plentiful pine.

BELFAST CITY

Balmoral
admin@balmoralgolf.com
www.balmoralgolf.com
Close by Belfast City centre and famous as long time home of the late Fred Daly, British Open champion in 1947.

Belvoir Park
info@belvoirparkgolfclub.com
www.belvoirpark.com
Product of the great architect Colt, one of finest inland courses in Ireland.

Castlereagh Hills
Exciting challenge in visitor-friendly surroundings.

Cliftonville
cliftonvillegolfclub@hotmail.co.uk
www.cliftonville.com
River presents just one of many hazards.

Colin Valley
colinvalleygolf@btconnect.com
Well-kept nine holes in wooded setting.

Dunmurray
dunmurraygc@hotmail.com
www.dunmurraygolfclub.co.uk
Much praised undulating mature venue with feature lake.

Fortwilliam
administrator@fortwilliam.co.uk
www.fortwilliam.co.uk
In midst of natural beauty of Cavehill and Belfast Lough, good experience through tree-lined fairways.

Knock
knockgolfclub@btconnect.com
Spreading trees, wide bunkers and ever present stream make for formidable test.

Malone
manager@malonegolfclub.co.uk
www.malonegofclub.co.uk
Supreme inland course amid mature woods, blazing flowers and with 25-acre trout-filled lake, by the side of which sits the feature 15th green.

Mount Ober
Mtober.gc@ukonline.co.uk
www.mountober.com
Seven par 3s, but no pushover.

Ormeau
Ormeau.golfclub@virgin.net
www.ormeaugolfclub.co.uk
Out of bounds a constant threat in lovely mature grounds within a drive and pitch of city.

Rockmount
rockmountgc@utvinternet.com
www.rockmountgolfclub.co.uk
Design brings out best of attractive natural features.

Shandon Park
shandonpark@btconnect.com
One of Northern Ireland's most popular clubs with clever mix of design concepts, especially on tougher front half.

COUNTY CAVAN

Belturbet
belturbet@golfnet.ie
Three par 3s provide extra spice to good value nine holes.

Blacklion
blackliongolfclub@yahoo.ie
www.blackliongolf.netfirms.com
Beautiful nine holes by lake.

Cabra Castle
etelectric@oceanfree.net
Scenic nine holes in grounds of hotel.

County Cavan
cavangolf@iol.ie;www.cavangolf.ie
Tough finishing stretch to one of Ireland's oldest courses, established in 1894.

Crover House
crover@iol.ie
www.croverhousehotel.ie
Nine holes, part of luxury hotel development beside Lough Sheelin.

Virginia
Enjoyable nine-hole option in leafy grounds of Park Hotel.

COUNTY DONEGAL

Ballybofey & Stranorlar
Superb views of Finn Valley and Donegal Mountains with premium on accurate tee shots.

Donegal
www.donegalgolfclub.ie
Also known as Murvagh, outstanding links situated on beautiful Murvagh Peninsula in Donegal Bay.

Buncrana
buncranagc@eircom.net
Superb nine-hole links, overlooking White Strand on Lough Swilly.

Bundoran
bundorangolfclub@eircom.net
www.bundorangolfclub.com
Fine course on cliff top with hotel facilities.

Cloughaneely
falcarraghgolfclub@eircom.net
Donegal's newest nine-hole course in grounds of historical Ballyconnell Estate with low green fee charges.

Cruit Island
cruitisland@eircom.net
Reputation spreading about merit of nine-hole cliff top links which has been a secret for too long!

Dunfanaghy
dunfanaghygolf@eircom.net
www.dunfanaghygolfclub.com
Steeped in history and showing all the character of legendary designer, Harry Vardon.

Greencastle
greencastlegolfclub@eircom.net
Peacefully sited in tranquil surroundings of Inishowen Peninsula.

Gweedore
Not too demanding nine hole links amidst Donegal Gaeltacht's magnificent vistas.

Letterkenny
letterkennygc@eircom.net
Beautiful parkland on shores of Lough Swilly with generous fairways flanked by mature foliage.

Nairn and Portnoo
nairnportnoo@eircom.net
www.nairnportnoogolfclub.ie
Challenging links in beautiful location.

North West
nwgchcap@iolfree.ie
Historic and venerable old links in constant war with coastal erosion.

Otway
Otway_golf_club@iolfree.ie
One of Ireland's oldest on shores of Lough Swilly.

Portsalon
portsalongolfclub@eircom.net
Classic old links offering stiff playing challenge.

Redcastle
redcastle.hotel@oceanfree.net
Top drawer nine holes on rising ground situated in hotel grounds on Inishowen Peninsula.

Rosapenna
rosapenna@eircom.net
www.rosapennagolflinks.ie
Old linksland pilgrim spot blessed by Old Tom Morris of St. Andrews; more recent work by Eddie Hackett and Pat Ruddy have combined to create 45-hole complex that sets it apart.

COUNTY DOWN

Ardglass
info@ardglassgolfclub.com
www.ardglassgolfclub.com
Stunning picture postcard links.

Ardminnan
Lesliejardine104@yahoo.co.uk
Featuring ponds in play on six of nine holes.

Banbridge
info@banbridge-golf.freeserve.co.uk
www.banbridge-golf.freeserve.co.uk
Lovely place to play in beautiful heart of Co. Down.

Bangor
admin@bangorgolfclubni.co.uk
www.bangorgolfclubni.co.uk
Championship parkland on rolling terrain with favourable reputation.

Blackwood
blackwoodgc@btopenworld.com
Course, plus par 3, and excellent practice amenities.

Bright Castle
Bright.castle@virgin.net
Four par 5s over 550 yards and one at 615 yards sets stern tone!

Carnalea
carnaleagolfclub@supanet.com
Short part links on shores of Belfast Lough.

Clandeboye
contact@cgc-ni.com
www.cgc-ni.com
Choice of shorter Ava or championship Dufferin courses in splendid raised setting amidst gorse.

Crossgar
crossgargolfclub@utvinternet.com
www.crossgargolfclub.co.uk
Short nine holes with four par 3s!

Donaghadee
deegolf@freenet.co.uk
Part links, part parkland with water hazards.

Downpatrick
office@downpatrickgolfclub.co.uk
www.downpatrickgolfclub.co.uk
Showing benefit of much repair work to complement setting beside Strangford Lough.

Edenmore
info@edenmore.com
www.edenmore.com
Prospering on the strength of many improvements.

Helen's Bay
mail@helensbaygc.com
Long established, short seaside nine holes of renown.

Hollywood
mail@hollywoodgolfclub.co.uk
www.hollywoodgolfclub.co.uk
Winding streams and trees add to difficult.

Kilkeel
www.kilkeelgolfclub.org
Another club to prosper by the design concept of Eddie Hackett.

Kirkistown Castle
kirkistown@supanet.com
www.linksgolfkirkistown.com
Maybe the most easterly sited club in Ireland – good links quality and splendid new clubhouse.

Mahee Island
Adrian.ross@ntlworld.com
www.maheeislandgolfclub.com
One of most scenic nine holes in Ireland. Test your skill at short 'Bird Island' eighth hole.

Mourne
andy@mournegc.freeserve.co.uk
www.mournegc.freeserve.co.uk
Warm and welcoming alongside austere Royal Co. Down.

Ringdufferin
mike@dallas102.freeserve.co.uk
Not too vigorously demanding but strong on scenery.

Royal Belfast
royalbelfastgc@btconnect.com
www.royalbelfast.com
Celebrated its centenary in 1981 as Ireland's oldest club, which enjoys serene setting falling gently to shores of Belfast Lough.

Scrabo
adminscrabogc@btinternet.com
www.scrabo-golf-club.org
Tough, tight test prospering in fabulous landscape.

Spa
spagolfclub@btconnect.com
www.spagolfclub.com
Tight in most parts on rising ground affording splendid views.

Temple
info@templegolf.com
www.templegolf.com
Double tee options combine to make for fulfilling golf in lovely surroundings.

Warrenpoint
office@warrenpointgolf.com
www.warrenpointgolf.com
Well-known and well-liked mature parkland with some great holes.

COUNTY FERMANAGH

Enniskillen
enniskillengolfclub@mail.com
www.enniskillengolfclub.com
Established in 1896, superb 18-hole parkland.

Lisnarick
lisnarick@golfnet.ie
Pleasant nine holes, inexpensive to play.

COUNTY DERRY

Brown Trout
bill@browntroutinn.com
www.browntroutinn.com
Beware - water in play at seven of nine holes!

Castlerock
info@castlerockgc.co.uk
castlerockgc.co.uk
Highly-regarded links with strong scenic qualities and many signature holes.

City of Derry
info@cityofderrygolfclub.com
www.cityofderrygolfclub.com
Busy 27-hole complex of repute overlooking River Foyle.

Faughan Valley
johncleghorn@faughanvalley.freeserve.co.uk
Short, picturesque parkland, inexpensive to play.

Foyle
foyle@golfnet.ie
www.foylegolfcentre.co.uk
Fine amenity includes championship standard course, nine hole par 3 and floodlit practice range.

Kilrea
www.kilreagolfclub.co.uk
Short nine-holer by standards but very pleasant to play.

Manor
Hasson320b@btopenworld.com
In grounds of grand old Victorian manor, rolling landscape offers good value for money.

Moyola Park
moyolapark@btconnect.com
Comfortably set into large acreage of wooded parkland split by River Moyola.

Portstewart
info@portstewartgc.co.uk
www.portstewartgc.uk
To refer only to the famous first hole is not to do full justice to a quite fabulous old links blended seamlessly into harmonising new terrain.

Roe Park
www.roepark.com
Mature sprawling hotel site lending itself ideally to golf.

Traad Ponds
Marvellous 9-hole green fee value on edge of Lough Neagh, abounding with wildlife.

COUNTY MONAGHAN

Castleblayney
castleblayney@golfnet.ie
www.castleblayneygolfclub.com
Low green fee located on shores of Lough Muckno in picturesque setting.

Clones
clonesgolfclub@eircom.net
www.clonesgolf.com
Reliably dry underfoot and offers good day's golf.

Mannan Castle
mannancastlegc@eircom.net
Good test of shot-making with half a dozen par 3s.

Nuremore
ldaly@ijm.ie
Quality hotel course, with strong water focal point.

Rossmore
rossmoregolfclub@eircom.net
www.rosssmoregolfclub.com
Des Smyth design in beautiful countryside with plenty of variety.

COUNTY TYRONE

Aughnacloy
tommystrain@btinternet.com
Nine holes in mature setting with river feature.

Benburb Valley
www.benburbvalley.co.uk
Sheltered nine holes flanked by River Blackwater with good off-course facilities.

Clogher Valley
info@cloghervalleygc.co.uk
www.cloghervalleygc.co.uk
Well laid out 9-hole pay-and-play club of highest quality.

Dungannon
info@dungannongolfclub.com
www.dungannongolfclub.com
Club that produced Ryder Cup star Darren Clarke, after whom the classic ninth hole is named.

Fintona
fintonagolfclub@tiscali.co.uk
If you don't get a birdie, you may catch a trout in the river that traverses most of the nine holes.

Killymoon
killymoongolf@btconnect.com
www.killymoongolf.com
Fairly flat parkland which presents varying challenge of six par 3s.

Newtownstewart
newtownstewart@lineone.net
www.globalgolf.com/newtownstewart.
Invigorating golf on rolling parkland of Baronscourt, ancestral estate of Duke of Abercorn.

Omagh
omaghgolfclub@tiscall.co.uk
Chip shot out of town comprising nines, separated by main road, one by the River Drumragh.

Strabane
strabanegc@btconnect.com
Along with River Mourne, includes an infamous par 3, known as The Graveyard!

Acknowledgements

The publisher thanks all the featured golf clubs and their staff for their assistance in the preparation of this book, including the provision of photographs and permission to reproduce them. The author also acknowledges the assistance of Damian Ryan (Fáilte Ireland), Paddy O'Looney (South West Ireland Golf), John McLoughlin (North and West Coast Links), An Post and Ms. Moira Cassidy (Portmarnock Links and Golf Hotel / East Coast Links). PICTURE CREDITS: photos.com, pp5, 130; Tim Hutchinson, pp5; Michael Diggin, pp6,13, 14,16, 26, 30, 34, 38, 44, 52, 58, 62, 79, 83bl, 85, 88, 89, 96, 102, 108, 122, 126, 140, 144, 145, 146, 148; © Matthew Harris/The Golf Picture Library, pp69, 71, 73, 74, 75, 86, 107, 108r, 110, 130r, 138; Michael Gill, pp68, 71b, 108bl, 112t, 112b, 114; Eric Hepworth, p132tl, Karl White, p16 and Fáilte Ireland, p90. Reproduction of First Day Cover by kind permission of An Post © 2005, p76.
Every effort has been made to locate and acknowledge owners of copyright material. However should any have been inadvertently missed the publishers will be pleased to make the usual arrangements upon notification.

This book was created by TONY POTTER PUBLISHING LTD, Haywards Heath, West Sussex, RH17 5PA. www.tonypotter.com.

DESIGN: Kevin Knight. EDITOR: Michael Gill.
DIAGRAMS AND CLUBHOUSE ILLUSTRATIONS: Jeremy Bays.
Published in Ireland by Gill and Macmillan Ltd.
Text © John Redmond 2006.
Format and design © Tony Potter Publishing Ltd 2006.
All rights reserved.

ISBN-13: 978 07171 4079 4   ISBN-10: 0 7171 4079 2